May this book be
a small present
to you from the
last six days war.
in Israel!
          Menachem Wakstok
             20.12. 67

# THE VICTORY

# THE VICT

## THE SIX-DAY

# ORY

## WAR OF 1967

| | |
|---|---|
| Editor: | Ohad Zmora |
| Text: | Raphael Bashan |
| Foreword: | Brig.-Gen. Haim Herzog |
| Translator: | Israel I. Taslitt |
| Layout: | Shmuel Brand |

 E. LEWIN-EPSTEIN LTD., PUBLISHERS

The photographs appearing in this volume were taken by Zahal (Israel Defense Forces) photographers in association with its Press Liaison Unit and the Government Press Office; "Newsphot"; "United Press International"; Boris Carmi; Dan Arazi (photos of and at the Western Wall); Don McCullin; Saadiah Mandel; Yitzhak Berez; Zvi Ron; Michael ben-Yossef; Aharon Lahav.
Maps: Press Liaison Unit of Zahal.
All rights reserved by E. Lewin-Epstein Ltd., Tel-Aviv, Publishers.
Photoset and printed in litho-offset by E. Lewin-Epstein Ltd., Bat-Yam, Israel.

## FOREWORD

*by General Haim Herzog*

DURING the year that preceded Israel's brilliant campaign, the Arab world kept toying with brinkmanship, pushing the situation to the very edge of the pit—but no farther. Especially adept at this game were the Syrians, who had the knack of not going beyond certain limits which would cause the conflagration they were provoking (on condition that others would do the fighting).

President Gamal Abdul Nasser of Egypt also moved cautiously. The presence of the United Nations Emergency Force (UNEF) at the Tiran Straits and along the common border with Israel gave him a convenient excuse for inaction.

May 1967 found Nasser at his lowest level in inter-Arab affairs; he had been warring with King Feisal of Saudi Arabia over control of Yemen and, after five years of fighting, could not point to any impressive gains. His economy was falling apart; relations with the U.S. were strained. The only country in the Arab Socialist camp on which he could still rely was Syria—the same Syria which had been doing everything to entangle Egypt in a struggle with Israel.

The telling Israeli response, on April 7, to the incidents inspired by Syria aroused deep concern among its leaders. Israel's reaction to the activities of the Syrian marauders made them stop and reconsider. In their consternation they called on Egypt, and their cry was echoed—as Nasser himself declared in his "resignation" speech—by the Russians, who confirmed Israel's "aggressive intent" toward Syria.

Nasser was faced with a dilemma. He finally decided that, if he would not rush to Syria's aid if she should be attacked by Israel, he would remain alone in the Arab world, ostracized and powerless. In mid-May he dispatched the bulk of the Egyptian forces to the Sinai Peninsula—a step sufficient in itself to cause a crisis. The Egyptian commander demanded of the UNEF commander that he concentrate his troops at a few points only, allowing Egypt to take over the others. Following an exchange of notes between Nasser and UN Secretary-General U Thant, the world suddenly learned that the UNEF had been withdrawn and that Israel now stood face to face with the Egyptian foe.

Nasser's declaration, closing the Straits of Tiran, followed. For years Israel had repeatedly stated that closing the Straits would mean war. The world's great powers had agreed with the principle involved, when Israel withdrew from Sharm-a-Sheikh in 1957. Nasser played this political card in the belief that he could thus tighten the noose around Israel's neck, perhaps even without a war, despite the warnings of the Israel Government. At this, Israel mobilized its armed forces and the home front, and awaited further developments.

The unbridled propaganda warfare waged by the Arabs reached unprecedented levels. The Arab world was promised victory, rape, murder, looting and spoils. Its imagination was fired with true Levantine ecstasy and delusions, and the Arab world—even a large segment of global public opinion—fully believed that, this time, victory would crown the Arab conquerors.

The stage was apparently set for the final, decisive act of the play authored by the fertile Arab imagination, with Israel, stripped of any tangible political support, completely alone against the armed Arab hordes. Uneasily, the world awaited what would come next. The Jewish people and Israel's friends were seized with alarm, while among its enemies great was the rejoicing.

Israel mobilized. Israel's security apparatus—a most amazing piece of machinery—went into high gear; quietly, confidently, engaging all the cogs—manpower, equipment, transport, electric power, supply, civil defense. Recalling, in its keen sense of history, that internal strife had been the ruination of the Second Commonwealth, the nation demanded that its leaders close political ranks and, as one, confront the foe. The response came quickly. Israel's leadership rose above partisan interests and brought forth national unity which, overnight, heightened the heart of every citizen with confidence, even optimism.

World Jewry suddenly understood that, without the State of Israel, its own existence would be bereft of meaning, that the fate of the Jewish people was inexorably bound up with the fate of Israel—and that Jews were indeed responsible for one another. Immediately, Israel was inundated with a wave of solidarity it had never before experienced. From wherever the Jewish heart was beating came volunteering, dedication and boundless love. Israel's populace discovered that the Jewish people was its sole dependable ally.

United and mobilized, Israel waited quietly, with full discipline and exemplary spirit. The diplomatic world pondered, held consultations—and came up with nothing. Arab hysteria kept mounting. Nasser could not afford to pass up the momentum. He promised the Arab people everything—and the Arab world waited.

The showdown came in the morning hours of Monday, June 5, 1967. It turned out to be one of the most glowing chapters in the war annals of the Jew—perhaps in all military history.

Jordan, now Egypt's puppet; Syria, cause of the conflagration, and Iraq, partner to the pact, now entered the field. Jordan brought the war to every home in Israel, as its forces sent shells screeching all along the border: new Jerusalem, Tel Aviv, Lydda Airport and the lowland settlements. The Syrians ceaselessly bombarded the settlements in the north. True to their promise, the Arabs now attacked from all sides.

Zahal (Israel Defense Forces) set the pace and the course of the fighting from its very beginning. Its three Commands—Southern, Central and Northern—were in full fighting array, prepared for any challenge. And in the first three hours of the war, in action unequalled in the history of air battle, the Israel Air Force gave Zahal complete air supremacy, making it possible for its commanders to unfold military operations under a steel umbrella which warded off any attack from above.

The amazing story of this war, the greatest miracle of this generation, is the subject of the following pages—the conquest of Sinai in sixty hours after the first contact with the enemy, the liberation of the West Bank and, above all, the redemption of Jerusalem the Indivisible, the removal of the Syrian threat from the northern settlements—to be told in the annals of the people of Israel for generations to come.

The most glorious single achievement was the restoration of Israel's crown to the head of its people. When Zahal's vaunted paratroopers broke through to the Wailing Wall and in tears leaned against its age-old stones—tough young men who had never prayed before in their lives—a great moment was inscribed in Jewish history, already replete with unforgettable moments of glory. An ancient prophecy has been fulfilled; the people of Israel will now dwell secure in its eternal capital.

Israel won because the people were united. Every soldier knew what was at stake. There was no alternative—had not been since the establishment of the State. And Israel knew how to build a superb military machine. Every detail had been planned to fit into the needs of any military action required. All these efforts—reserves, mobilization techniques, national resources—justified themselves when the fateful hour struck.

Zahal's ceaseless stress on air and armored power also proved its validity. These two arms of Israel's battle array made victory certain. Zahal faced some of the most modern weapons in the world today—and bested them.

But foremost and above everything else, Zahal was able to train, over the years, a generation of exemplary commanders who enjoyed the boundless trust of their men. This is the greatest asset that any army can have. The Israeli commander has always gone first, leading his troops. In the thickest of fighting he never abandons his post unless he is wounded, and his soldiers abandon neither him nor each other.

The proportion of officers in the total number of casualties is about two and a half times the proportion elsewhere. This, too, is a secret of Zahal's success in battle.

The political map of the Middle East and the entire world was altered overnight. The Russians, having succeeded after centuries' long efforts to establish themselves in the Mediterranean and Red Seas, "contributed" quite a bit to the outbreak of hostilities. In Syria they side-stepped NATO and CENTO, while in Egypt and Yemen they found confederates who provided them with a beachhead on both Seas. The West witnessed these political developments in blank wonder, devoid of any definite policy or long-range political thinking. The oil treasures of the Persian Gulf and the Arabian Desert were endangered.

The annihilation of Israel planned by the Arab forces and abetted by the Soviet Union would have caused global upheaval. It would have thrust the entire Middle East, western Asia and most of the African continent into the Soviet sphere of influence. The pawn was far greater than the State of Israel itself; it was the control over a substantial portion of the globe. But the coveted prize was denied them by an army of reservists operating with trucks ordinarily used for delivering milk, vegetables or groceries.

Zahal's triumph changed the political complexion of Israel and the entire world. Israel reached boundaries never before held by the people of Israel during its long history. A boundary is essentially an expression of political, military and economic exigencies. While these boundaries are now the subject of international pressure, Israel cannot afford to be oblivious to these exigencies. Sharm-a-Sheikh is vital to Israel's geopolitical and economic location. That the border with Jordan should again permit violence against Israel's capital and cities is unthinkable. Equally out of the question is the assumption that the settlements opposite the Syrian highlands should be abandoned to the whims of every Syrian dictator.

Israel is now entrenched along the length and breadth of its new borders. This is a fact. If the Arab world wants peace, there will be peace. If not—Israel has lived and grown and prospered, to this day, without it. Israel can now afford to wait.

All this we have achieved at great cost—the heart's blood of the flower of our youth. Their sacrifice must not be in vain.

**THE DARK**

IT may well be that none of the two hundred thousand spectators at the Zahal (Israel Defense Forces) Independence Day Parade of 1967 in Jerusalem, nor anyone among the thousands listening to its broadcast account at home, would have imagined that those tanned and stalwart young men, marching with heads high in precise formation, would, within a month, be going forth to do battle with four Arab armies and would, in a campaign without precedent, transform Israel's borders beyond recognition—stretching from Egypt's fortifications at the Suez Canal to the Syrian bunkers in the highlands of Golan, from Jordanian pillboxes in Old Jerusalem to the distant Straits of Tiran.

As always, Independence Day celebrations this year topped all other festivities. In Jerusalem floodlights illuminated the Night

# DAYS OF CRISIS

Tatoo. In Haifa, the sound of merry-making floated out across the Bay. In Tel-Aviv, scores of popular entertainers made the rounds from one open-air stage to another, and thirty-two mobile children were returned to their frantic parents by the police. Five men of letters were awarded the Israel Prize, an annual feature of the Day.

But alongside the reports on the festivities in the newspapers a word of warning crept in: Egypt was parading troops through Cairo and out to the highway going east— to Sinai. Foreign correspondents cabled the account: truckloads of steel-helmeted troops, hundreds of tanks, field and anti-aircraft artillery, jeeps and ambulances— heading east. Cairo's most influential daily, *El Ahram*, informed its readers that Egypt was taking precautions against an Israeli attack.

Israel kept a wary eye on the Egyptian advance toward its borders, but it remained calm. Experts stated, via the press, that "the Egyptian move is just so much muscle-flexing designed to put pressure on Israel," merely a show of force with no aggressive intent behind it. Commentators on Middle East affairs were certain that Egypt was pointing up the situation in the area, in case Israel was considering retaliation for Syria's unremitting acts of terror.

Egypt kept stoking the propaganda boilers. Egyptian forces were rolling steadily toward the Gaza Strip and eastern Sinai; Egypt's civil defense had been put on a 24-hour alert; meetings were being held without let-up with brother diplomats of Arab states and the Soviet Union; communiques always ended on the same note—Israel must be annihilated.

To all this, Zahal's comment was brief and restrained: "Zahal is following developments closely and is aware of what is taking place."

Throughout Israel life was routine. *El Fatah* marauders, operating this time out of Jordan, committed two more acts of sabotage; "Israel has submitted a complaint to the Mixed Armistice Commission." At the meeting of the Government, Prime Minister Levi Eshkol made note of the increase of Egyptian forces in Sinai. Consensus: "Propaganda aside, we must take into account the practical implications of this change in the balance of strength in the south."

On the next day (Wednesday, two days after Independence Day), Egypt's President made the second move in his chess game. In a neat manouver, the UNEF was eased out of its bases along the Israeli frontier and had to restrict itself to the Gaza Strip on the coast. The Egyptian Chief-of-Staff, General Mahmoud Fawzi, wired UNEF's commander, General Rikkiyeh of India: "I have instructed the Egyptian forces to be prepared for action against Israel as soon as she commits an act of aggression against any Arab state. Please withdraw the UNEF from Sinai forthwith so that the safety of your men may be assured."

To everyone's surprise, UN Secretary-General U Thant complied immediately. Since the UNEF is in the area only because the Egyptian Government had allowed it, the demand for withdrawal must necessarily be obeyed. The explanation was received

EGYPTIAN VEHICLES ROLL ALONG SINAI ROUTES.

NASSER'S COMMANDOS DISPLAY THEIR PROWESS.

ENTHUSED EGYPTIANS ARM FOR "HOLY WAR".

GIANT HELICOPTERS AIRLIFT TROOPS TO SINAI.

CAIRO WANTS BLOOD.    "PALESTINE" LINEUP.

in Israel with disgust; elsewhere it earned an uneasy shrug. Later it was said that the man on the 38th floor of the UN Building had based his act on the assumption that Nasser did not really mean war and would therefore refrain from asking for complete evacuation. If so, Mr. U Thant was mistaken. Within 24 hours the Egyptian delegate to the UN handed the Secretary-General a sealed demand that the UNEF withdraw completely. Out!

In Egypt itself, the sabre-rattling grew louder. Egypt's Vice-President Marshal Amer flew to an advance air base in Sinai "for consultation". General Murtaghi was appointed commander of the "Israel Frontier Forces". Damascus Radio reported: "The Syrian army is on full alert." The head of the Jordan Government, announcing the concentration of its forces along the Israel border, said: "The armistice lines of all the Arab states are now one line. Aggression against one state will be considered an attack against all of us." Nor does Iraq stand aloof; it announces its readiness to dispatch an army force and aircraft to Syria.

While U Thant is packing his valises in New York for his flight to Cairo, the UNEF, acting on his instructions, is vacating the seventy-three posts along the entire length of the Egypt–Israel border which it had occupied since the Sinai Campaign of 1956. The abandoned posts are immediately taken over by Ahmed Shukeiry's "Palestine Liberation Organization." An Egyptian force with long-range artillery moves into the UN quarters at Sharm-a-Sheikh, commanding the Straits of Tiran. In Israel, the citizenry wakes up to find that the milkman, the newsdealer, the bank clerk have all disappeared. The reserves have been mobilized.

Western circles attempt to reassure Israel. After all, Nasser is tied up in Yemen . . . Russia cannot possibly be interested in a Middle East clash . . . Egypt is simply demonstrating its support of Syria . . . Sharm-a-Sheikh is just another set on the stage where Nasser is play-acting.

But Egypt talks and acts differently. Marshal Amer: "Israel's recent declarations are too arrogant to be ignored. Israel, the tool of imperialism and reaction, believes that the engagement of Egyptian forces in Yemen is restraining our hand, but our concentration in Sinai, in unprecedented strength, can repel any Israeli threat and deal the enemy a mortal blow."

The U.S., Canada, France and Britain are openly critical of U Thant's hasty and incomprehensible move. Britain's Foreign Minister George Brown states bluntly that evacuation of the UNEF forces at such a time turns UN peace-keeping action into shameful mockery.

World capitals are busy conjecturing, commenting, advising, groping, prophesying.

IN ISRAEL: MOBILIZATION, BRIEFING, FULL ALERT.

UNEF EVACUATES GAZA STRIP, WHICH IS THEN TAKEN OVER BY AHMED SHUKEIRY'S MEN.

TIRAN STRAITS ARE CLOSED. EGYPTIANS RE-ESTABLISH BASE AT SOUTHERN TIP OF PENINSULA (SHARM-A-SHEIKH).

NAHAL OZ WHEAT FIELDS AFIRE. SHELLING FROM STRIP ENDS TEN YEARS OF TRANQUILITY.

MARSHAL AMER AT EGYPTIAN AIRBASE: "ALOFT, O EAGLES! . . . LIBERATE RAVISHED PALESTINE!".

JORDAN LEGION IS UNITED AND READY.

EGYPTIANS JEER AT U.S. SHIP EN ROUTE THROUGH SUEZ CANAL

U Thant swallows diplomatic affront from Nasser, gets appointment but no concession.

King Hussein and Big Brother Nasser.

Shukeiry is sure annihilation of Israel is here.

Effigies hanged in Cairo.

Milan's influential *Corriere della Sera* quotes the experts: "The feeling in Israel is that Nasser is merely trying to smooth Syria's ruffled feathers and to control the activities of the Palestinian marauders. On the other hand, who knows where such tactics end and the crisis in the big Mid-East poker game begins!" Correspondents of leading newspapers in Turkey, France and England cable from Cairo and Beirut that the whole thing is but a storm in a teacup.

In Israel, the last traces of faith in the UN are fading quickly. Foreign Minister Abba Eban convenes the foreign ambassadors and announces that Israel takes strong exception to the evacuation of the UNEF, in which it sees a change in the status quo. The Government is now studying the inevitable implications of this precipitous action.

While the clouds gather, Israel calmly pursues its daily life. President Zalman Shazar is off on a three-week visit to Canada, Iceland and Scotland; the foreign trade imbalance has been reportedly reduced; two players of Israel's All-Star soccer team are fined for not showing up for training on time, and the twentieth child of Mrs. Amalia Ben-Harush, born in Haifa on the eve of Independence Day, has been duly circumcized and given the name "Yisrael."

But in diplomatic circles the Middle East situation has taken on the shape of a powder keg. The Security Council convenes. The discussions are long and sterile; the delegates from East European states, inspired by the Soviet Union, sabotage every attempt to solve the problem. In Jerusalem the conviction grows that Israel cannot rely for its survival on any outside factors.

The first Sabbath of the crisis (May 20) was ushered in with news that Egypt was calling up its reserves . . . the Jordanian Chief-of-Staff has arrived in Cairo . . . the U.S. Sixth Fleet is on its way to the eastern Mediterranean . . . Shukeiry is planning to increase fedayyin activity inside Israel's borders. Still, Israel's Prime Minister tells the Knesset on the next day that, while Zahal is ready for any eventuality, Israel is hopeful of peace and is ready to join in any attempt to maintain it.

The UN Secretary-General alighted at Cairo airport in the morning hours of Wednesday, May 24. Nasser marked his arrival by advancing the crisis another notch; he closed the Straits of Tiran. Flambuoyantly he states: "Under no circumstances will I suffer the Israeli flag in the Gulf of Akaba! The Straits are in the territorial waters of Egypt! We shall not give up a grain of sand. The Jews are threatening us with war; we reply, then: Come on! Egypt is ready!"

In Israel the air of serenity has vanished. Signs of the crisis are everywhere: hardly any young men in the streets; people are going about grim-lipped, carrying blackout paper and rolls of gummed tape; nervous housewives sweep the grocery shelves clean of essential and other commodities . . . candles, matches, flashlight and transistor batteries outstrip everything except sugar and rice; Britain and the U.S. advise their nationals to leave; the Hungarian State Circus and Conductor Eric Leinsdorf leave in the middle of their engagements; Met favorites Roberta Peters and Richard Tucker decide to stick it out "as long as the need is there"; Conductor Zubin Mehtah and artists all over the world— Jews and non-Jews—offer to cancel their contracts elsewhere and come to Israel. Abroad, young and old besiege Israel diplomatic centers, college diplomas in some hands, each volunteering to serve in the capacity for which he is best suited. Correspondents of the world's newspapers and wire services begin converging on Jerusalem.

Diplomatic activity is at last-ditch height. Foreign Minister Eban leaves for France and England to clarify Israel's stand as well as feel the pulse at the Quay d'Orsay and 10 Downing Street. Help may be given, he is told, "if Israel does not commit any warlike act." So much for that.

Nasser, having allowed U Thant to cool

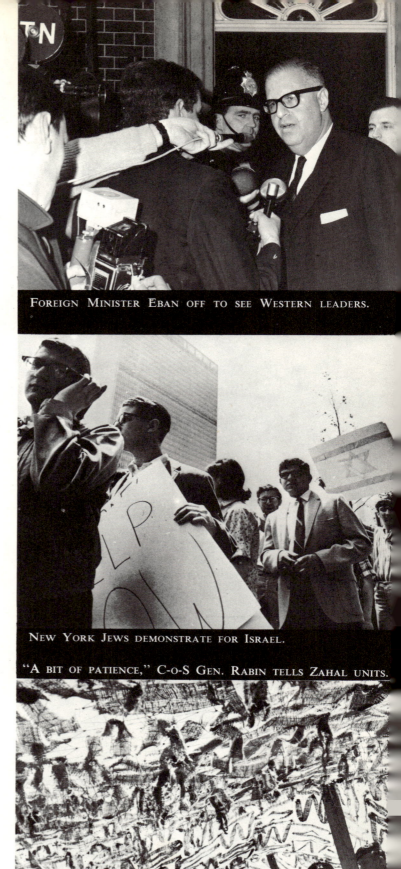

FOREIGN MINISTER EBAN OFF TO SEE WESTERN LEADERS.

NEW YORK JEWS DEMONSTRATE FOR ISRAEL.

"A BIT OF PATIENCE," C-o-S GEN. RABIN TELLS ZAHAL UNITS.

UN SECURITY COUNCIL convenes, converses, disperses.

JEWISH VOLUNTEERS arrive at LYDDA.

LONDON demands action in ISRAEL'S behalf.

PARIS demands that FRANCE keep faith with ISRAEL.

ISRAEL'S UNITED GOVERNMENT holds first session.

NEW DEFENSE MINISTER MAJ.-GEN. MOSHE DAYAN AND C-O-S GEN. RABIN.

his heels in Cairo for 24 hours, finally agrees to see the Secretary-General. At this point, no one believes any longer that Nasser will back down on the Straits of Tiran. On the contrary, intoxicated with his own diplomatic progress, he decrees that the Straits are mined and that fire will be opened on any ship flying the Israeli flag attempting to get through. The Security Council convenes, converses and disperses.

In Israel, many feel that the time element is working to the disadvantage of the State. The initiative has now been lost, they claim. Government officials argue that all possible diplomatic means must first be exhausted. On the same day, Saudi Arabia, Jordan and Egypt proclaim total mobilization. Civil defense workers in Tel-Aviv check air-raid shelters for full and instant use. Universities cancel classes; the lecturers have been called up. Long queues line up at bus stops, vainly waiting for buses whose drivers are on military duty. *Magen David Adom* ambulances are taking blood from thousands on street corners. Money, valuables, taxes not yet due pour in.

The diplomatic cauldron keeps boiling. Russia rejects Gen. De Gaulle's offer to have the Four Powers mitigate the crisis. Egypt's Defense Minister Badran is in Moscow for secret talks. Minister Eban sees Secretary Dean Rusk twice, and his meeting with President Johnson is second-guessed all around the globe.

May 27—the second Sabbath of the crisis. Abba Eban is back from Washington. Nothing concrete, it seems, except for President Johnson's promise to push unequivocally for a just and permanent solution to the innocent passage of all ships through the waters of Tiran. Nasser warns that if the West intervenes he will shut down the Suez Canal while other Arab states will shut off the flow of oil to Europe. Units from Kuwait reach Cairo, all set "to defend the great Arab fatherland." In New York, 100,000 Jews march in a demonstration of solidarity with Israel. Hundreds of newsmen and television crews are becoming restless: "Where's the war?"

On May 30, the Prime Minister tells the Knesset: "Free passage through the Straits of Tiran and the Gulf of Eilat is of primary national interest on which there can be no compromise and from which there can be no retreat." But U.S. public opinion does not believe that the issue is worth a war. In Paris, Baron Edmund de Rothschild raises in a few days two million dollars for Israel's defense effort, a sum greater than what France had raised during the entire year.

Egypt sticks to the course it had charted. At 12:30 p.m. on May 30, civilian farmers in the fields of Nahal-Oz come under a hail of machine-gun and mortar fire from the Gaza Strip. Hundreds of acres of ripe wheat are set aflame.

The coil of enemy strength around Israel continues to tighten, and now the last link in the chain is forged: King Hussein of Jordan shows up in Cairo unexpectedly. With him are his Prime Minister, his Chief-of-Staff, and "Palestine Liberation Organization" manager Ahmed Shukeiry. They go into an excited huddle with Nasser, and an official statement emerges: "Egypt and Jordan have signed a three-year mutual defense pact ... Should war break out, the commander of the Egyptian forces will also command the Jordanian Legion." Affixing his signature, Nasser solemnly declares: "We are facing a fateful challenge on the part of not only Israel but also of those who stand behind her—the U.S. and Britain! ... The combined military might of Egypt, Syria, Lebanon and Jordan is now arrayed along the borders of Israel, supported by forces from Iraq, Algeria, Kuwait and Sudan! ... The problem is no longer that of the Gulf of Akaba but of Palestine itself!"

Those in charge of Israel's security were quick to grasp the significance of the Egypt–Jordan pact. It meant new tension along Israel's longest border with an Arab country, a border furthermore topographically and strategically weak. Along this border, now that the pact had been signed, would be deployed Iraqi forces—a gross violation of the status quo in a sector where the Israel Government had declared it would act as it saw fit.

Israel's response to the pact was the unification of its Government; all the major parties now participated in setting policy. At Lydda International Airport El Al Airlines kept discharging capacity loads of Israelis returning for service. Lieut. Amnon Dehan decided to name his newly-born son "Tiran."

Chief-of-Staff Maj.-Gen. Yitzhak Rabin

asked his officers and soldiers for "a bit of patience." While Zahal is capable, he said, of beating the enemy on its own territory, the political and military arenas are two arms of the same body. "The transition from one to the other can be sharp and sudden. Let us not delude ourselves into thinking that the danger has diminished ...

I know that the effort for a soldier to wait under high tension is no lighter than it is in actual combat."

The U.P. correspondent in Cairo quotes reliable sources that Egypt, Jordan and Syria have a joint plan for a lightning attack on Israel by land, sea and air; objective: to wipe out Israel in a matter of hours, should it open fire against any Arab state.

On June 2 the unified Government comes into being. Maj.-Gen. Moshe Dayan is now Minister of Defense; Menahem Begin and Yosef Sapir, ministers without portfolio. While Israel's citizens and soldiers cheer, the outside world forebodingly mutters that "extremists in Israel have been strengthened ... Israel's stand is bound to be much tougher." *L'Aurore* (Paris) comments: "Nasser and Shukeiry should now rethink their plans. With Dayan the Minister of Defense there will be a countdown—to zero!"

On June 4, President De Gaulle announces that France will remain neutral in the looming Mediterranean conflict. Whoever would fire the first shot would topple from French grace. In Israel, this declaration causes astonishment and disappointment, not unmixed with disgust.

At his first press conference, the new Minister of Defense, replying to a question about the time element, has this to say: "I don't believe that nations can live with a stop-watch in hand, and that if anything goes awry the entire nation will crumble. There are more preferable and less preferable situations. The question is how the time is being used. Our situation a month hence may be even better—if we use the time for things which will improve our situation. Time causes change—what we do with it is what's important."

# BREAKTHROUGH DAY

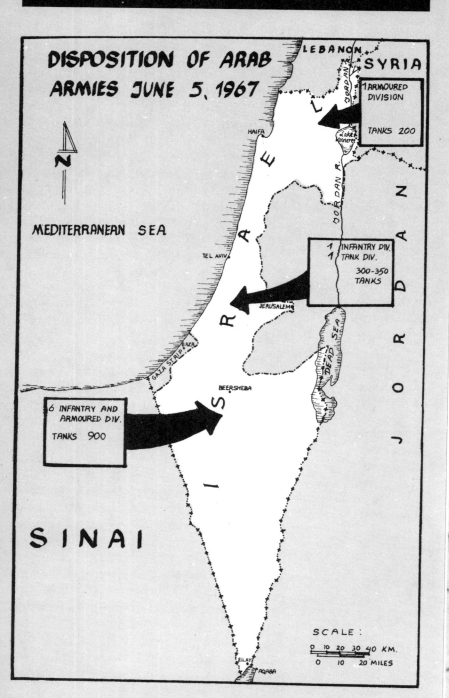

DISPOSITION OF ARAB
ARMIES JUNE 5, 1967

LEBANON

SYRIA

1 ARMOURED
DIVISION

TANKS 200

N

MEDITERRANEAN SEA

HAIFA

Lake Kinneret

I S R A E L

TEL AVIV

1 INFANTRY DIV.
1 TANK DIV.

300-350
TANKS

JERUSALEM

GAZA STRIP

DEAD SEA

J O R D A N

BEERSHEBA

6 INFANTRY AND
ARMOURED DIV.

TANKS 900

SINAI

SCALE:
0 10 20 30 40 KM.
0 10 20 MILES

EILAT
AQABA

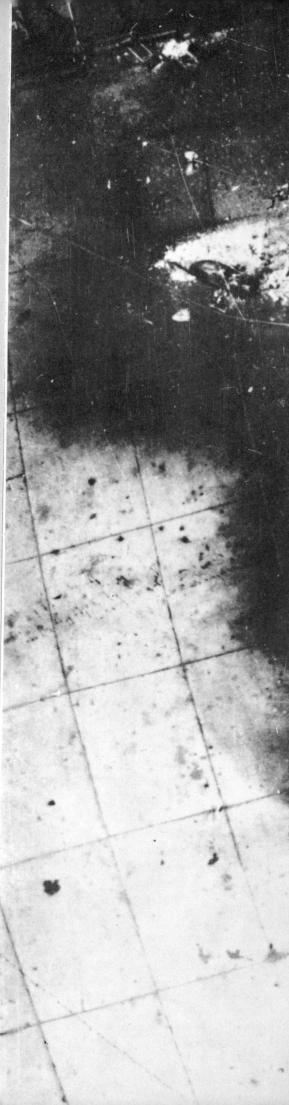

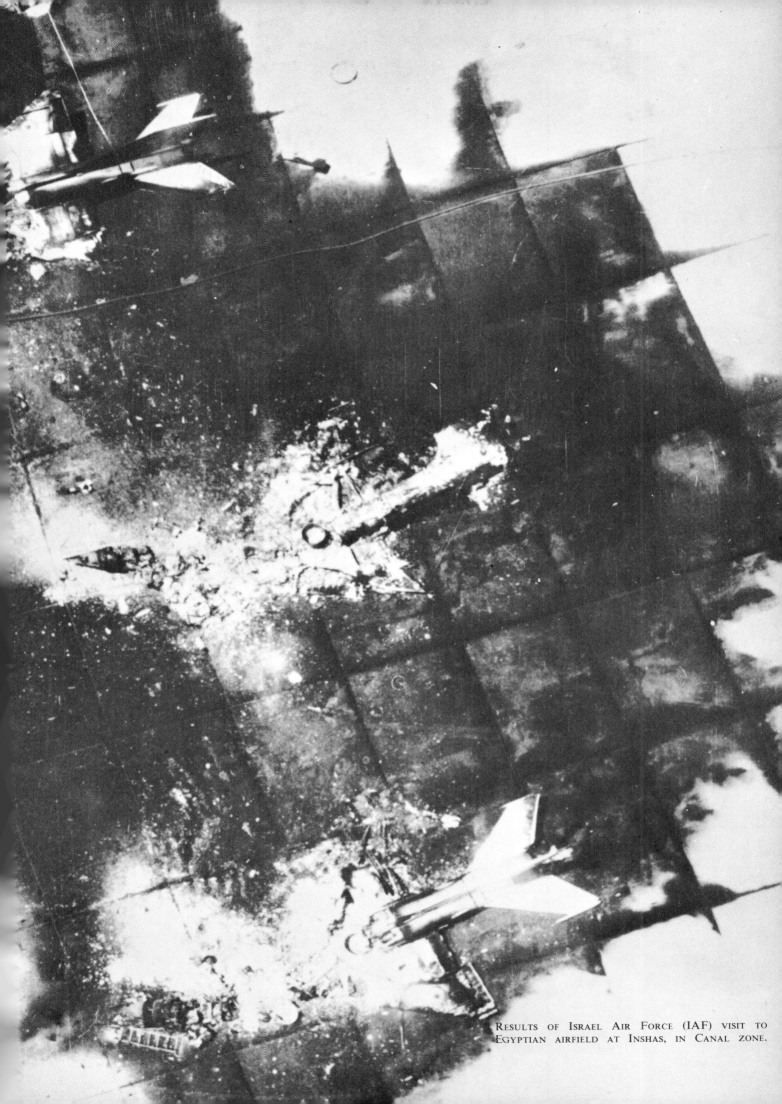

RESULTS OF ISRAEL AIR FORCE (IAF) VISIT TO EGYPTIAN AIRFIELD AT INSHAS, IN CANAL ZONE.

"THE FIELD WAS SO OVERCAST WITH SMOKE WE COULDN'T FIND A TARGET."

"MIRAGE" FIGHTERS STREAK TOWARD TARGETS: EGYPT'S AIRFIELDS.

DAWN on Monday, June 5, brought no comfort to Israel's populace. The morning papers noted the Government's concern over the snail-like pace of international action on the Tiran blockade . . . Egypt and Iraq had signed a formal mutual defense pact . . . Egypt was air-lifting artillery and troops to Jordan . . . Damascus announced the deployment of Iraqi troops along the West Bank, all the way down to Hebron . . . Arab oil-producing countries were talking in Baghdad about banning shipments to consignees friendly to Israel. More Soviet battleships had passed through the Bosphorus, and Red China was offering aid to Egypt. Jordanian positions in Jerusalem had begun shooting.

And yet, there were also a few pinpoints of light: a million telegrams urging support of Israel had already been delivered at the White House in Washington . . . Airports from London to Sydney, from Paris to Johannesburg were jammed with hundreds of young Jewish volunteers waiting for the first opportunity to come to Israel . . . All now felt it, the hearts of Jews everywhere beating in solidarity with beleaguered Israel. Statesmen, academicians, newspapers and organizations throughout the world, from near and far, from all segments of the community, continue proclaiming their support of Israel. Jorja Luis Burjas, the most outstanding author of Argentina, declared his undivided support of Israel before the press. Wrote the German *Bild Zeitung:* "If the free world does not arise and stand up against the Egyptian blockade of Eilat, then the Soviets will be able to blockade Berlin—or any other place in the world." In Vienna, a declaration of deep support of Israel, signed by more than 100 intellectuals and presented to the head of the Austrian Government, was given wide circulation among the public. The *Journal da Brazil* and the *Astro da San Paolo*, two of Brazil's largest newspapers, strongly attacked Nasser. In Freetown, capital of Sierra Leone, a delegation of the National Youth Movement visited the Israeli Embassy and informed the Ambassa-

ONE OF EGYPT'S MAJOR AIRFIELDS IS SCENE OF UTTER HAVOC:
BURNING PLANES, TWISTED WRECKAGE, RIPPED RUNWAYS.

FOUR GIANT MY-6 'COPTERS DESTROYED AT BIR-GAFGAFA (ONE IS SHROUDED BY SMOKE).

dor of its decision to support Israel in its justified struggle against Arab imperialism.

At 7:55 a.m., the air attack warning sirens went off in Tel-Aviv. People hurried into the shelters, poked their heads out, scanned the skies. No sound overhead. "A mistake. Someone got nervous and pushed the button."

But fifteen minutes later, *Kol Yisrael* newscaster Yoram Arbel stated the facts:

"Zahal's spokesman has informed us that, since early this morning, pitched battles have been going on in the southern sector between Egyptian air and armor and Zahal forces. Our radar has also picked up Egyptian jets heading for the Israel coast and the Negev. The Israel Air Force has gone out to meet them, and the battle is still going on."

"Still going on". . . *Kol Yisrael* newscasts, now on the air every hour, continue to be

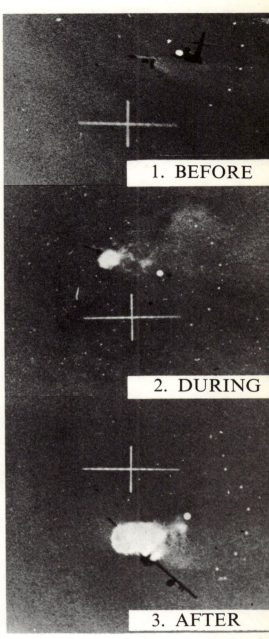

1. BEFORE

2. DURING

3. AFTER

SECTION OF CAIRO, EGYPT'S CAPITAL, SEEN THROUGH IAF LENS.

IAF PLANE HAS MIG IN ITS SIGHTS.

veiled. "Tank and air battles are still taking place in the south." The home front grows uneasy. At 9:20 Cairo Radio blares forth: "Arise! Go forth into battle! The hour of glory is here!"

9:25 a.m. The French news agency in Cairo reports air raid sirens and heavy explosions in the area. Damascus Radio adds its bit: "The time has come! Silence the enemy! Destroy him! Liberate Palestine!"

9:40 a.m. Cairo Radio reports, officially,

that Israel has launched an attack on Egypt by land and air. Cairo calls on Jordan and Syria to enter the fray.

9:50 a.m. Damascus Radio: "We are now in the thick of battle."

10:00 a.m. Cairo Radio: "Pounce forward, O mighty eagles of ours! See you in Tel-Aviv!" Baghdad Radio reports a Foreign Ministry announcement to the effect that Egyptian airfields are under attack.

In Israel, where broadcasts in Arabic are

CHARRED EVIDENCE OF ZAHAL'S SUCCESSFUL BREAKTHROUGH TO GAZA.

understood by half the populace, nerves strained to the breaking point. "What's going on? Why is no information coming over *Kol Yisrael*? What is happening in the south?" At 10:00 a.m. Gen. Ezer Weizmann, Chief of Operations of the General Staff, asks reservists to report to the following units: "Love of Zion", "The Last of the Just", "Close Shave", "Alternating Current", "Matador", "Deep Roots", "Gates of Salvation", "Pure Quartz", "Men of Toil", "Wedding March", "Silver Lining". . .

The first bit of real news comes, strangely enough, from Paris. Reuter quotes the Israel Embassy press officer as saying that Israel had already put 117 Egyptian aircraft out of commission. *Kol Yisrael* announces, in its Arabic broadcast, that more than 120 Egyptian planes had been destroyed. But Zahal cautions: "The news made public supposedly by the Israel Embassy in Paris and by *Kol Yisrael* in Arabic, concerning heavy losses by the Egyptian Air Force are premature, unverified, and highly unreliable."

Once again the gloom of uncertainty shrouds Israel. Ears grow hot against the transistors.

10:40 a.m. The quiet and reserved voice of Defense Minister Moshe Dayan: "Soldiers of Zahal! At this moment we are still without exact information on the battles in progress along the southern front. Our planes are engaging enemy aircraft in bitter fighting. Our ground forces have gone forth to silence Egyptian artillery, now heavily shelling our settlements opposite the Gaza Strip, and to check the Egyptian armored force now driving to cut off the southern portion of the Negev.

"General Murtaghi of Egypt, commander of the Arab forces in Sinai, has sent a radio message to his soldiers, telling them that the eyes of the entire world are upon them for the results of the holy war. He has asked them to achieve victory by force of arms and in solidarity with the 'ravished soil of Palestine.'

"Soldiers of Zahal! We do not aim at conquest. Our sole objective is to put to naught

FOUGA-MAGISTERS STRAFE EGYPTIAN POSITIONS.

Zahal armor seals off escape route for Egyptian tanks in Gaza.

Egyptian train, laden with military equipment and supplies, is riddled like a sieve.

Medical Corps helicopters evacuate wounded. Swift transfer to hospitals saved many lives.

Zahal units take a breather near Khan-Yunis mosque.

the attempt by Arab forces to conquer our land. We seek to break and destroy the ring of blockade and aggression surrounding us. The Egyptians have enlisted the aid, and have assumed command, of the forces of Syria, Jordan and Iraq. These have been joined by units from Kuwait and Algeria. They outnumber us, but we shall overcome them. We are a small nation, but undaunted; loving peace, yet prepared to fight for its life and land.

"The home front will certainly do its share to bear the burden. But the main effort will be up to you, the soldiers, fighting in the air, on land and sea, they who man the trenches in the border settlements and they who mount the tank attacks.

"Soldiers of Zahal! Today our hope and trust is with you."

Prime Minister Levi Eshkol broadcasts to the nation: "We shall repulse the enemy and vanquish his forces. United and strong, we shall stand fast in the struggle that has been forced upon us."

A new prayer for the day by the Chief Chaplain, Brigadier-General Shlomo Goren; quoting from the Bible: "Thus shall all Thy foes perish, O Lord, and Israel will dwell secure in its land, spreading to the west and to the east, to the north and to the south."

The special editions of the noon papers can draw only a vague verbal outline of the battlefront. Zahal had made contact with the Egyptian forces; a heavy battle between armored units is taking place at Khan-Yunis in the Gaza Strip. Details are still unavailable, and the pall hangs on.

10:10 a.m. Damascus Radio: "The Syrian Air Force is attacking Israel."

11:15 a.m. Cairo Radio (in Hebrew): "The full-scale war against Israel has been launched." 11:30 a.m. "O ye Arabs! For the sake of our honor, history, present and future, we are now waging the critical struggle. Let us shatter Israel's perfidious attack!" 1:50 p.m. "Egypt has formally notified the President of the Security Council that Israel had committed aggression by attacking planes and airfields."

In Tel-Aviv people shuttle back and forth from warning to all-clear. Exhortations from Cairo and Damascus grow in vehemence: "O ye Arabs! Soon we shall return to the captive homeland! Yes, yes! See you in Tel-Aviv!" To which *Kol Yisrael* replies in equally descriptive Arabic: "O ye Arabs! Your leaders are dragging you off to disaster! This is your opportunity to rid yourselves of oppressive regimes! This is the hour to demolish the hated hierarchy! Nasser wanted to give you war—now you have it! Zahal, victorious in the past, will triumph again. While there is still time, rise and rebel against Abdul Nasser!"

Cairo Radio announces the aerial bombardment of the Egyptian positions at Sharm-a-Sheikh. The A.P. correspondent in the Old City reports that fighting has broken out all along the Jordanian border; the news remains unverified, but the first

SINAI PENINSULA

LEGEND
INTERNATIONAL BOUNDARY
ARMISTICE DEMARCATION LINE
MAIN LINES OF COMMUNICATION
SCALE
0 10 20 40 60 80
KILOMETERS

◄ A NAP IN THE SHADE OF A HALF-TRACK.

JORDANIANS BOMB NETANYA AREA. TWO OF THE WOUNDED. - JORDANIAN SHELLING HITS ALONG ENTIRE BORDER.

air raid warning had already sounded in Jerusalem at 11:30 that morning.

King Hussein of Jordan had cast his lot.

Not content with firing a few perfunctory shots, as so many had thought he would do, he plunged into the conflict full-force. At 11:45 a.m., the Jordanians began shelling Mt. Scopus and Ramat Rahel, and at the same time their artillery opened with flat trajectory bombardment across No Man's Land separating the Old City from the New.

The shelling now straddles the entire Israel–Jordan boundary line. 12:15 a.m.—Jordanian "Hunter" planes attack Netanya, on the seacoast. Three Syrian MIG-17's bomb Megiddo and are felled by IAF fighter planes. 12:30 a.m.—Syrian planes bomb the Haifa Bay area, including the Arab village of Elbon. The shelling goes on without letup. Egyptian General Abdul Muneim Riad, head of the Joint Arab Command, is directing the Jordanian moves; he wants to whip up as much turmoil as possible in this sector in order to force Zahal to keep much of its strength

here and thus relieve the pressure on the Egyptians in Sinai.

The Jordanians are on a rampage of shooting, shelling, bombing. They turn automatic fire on Sandala Village in the Afula sector; three Jordanian "Hunters" bomb the Kaplan Quarter in the Kfar Saba area, killing four and wounding fifteen. A Syrian MIG was observed falling in the Toufik area. At 1:00 p.m. a Jordanian force breaks into the High Commissioner's Palace in the demilitarized zone, chases away the small force of the UN Mixed Armistice Commission, and tries to advance toward the agricultural school in Ramat Rahel. Zahal came back with a counterattack, and in a short but bitter fight regained the Palace. More to the south, the Jordanians sent shells flying toward Nehusha in the Lakhish area. Ten persons were injured by Jordanian fire near the Italian Hospital in Jerusalem. Shells tear gaping holes in the Nahlat Shim'on, Meah-Shearim and Musrara quarters in the capital. No part of the long border between Jordan and Israel is spared. Lahav in the southern Negev is hit, Tirat-Zvi in the Beisan Valley sector; Nahal Oz

PARATROOPERS AND GEAR READY TO BOARD FOR DESTINATION.

is hit from the Gaza Strip; Syria shells Rosh-Pinna.

Night brings no respite. At 7:30 p.m. Jordanian long-range artillery reaches Tel-Baruch beach, Lydda, Netanya, Kfar Sirkin. At 9:15 they reach Tel-Aviv, scoring a direct hit on a residence in Masaryk Square. The citizens of Israel's largest metropolis now know that the war has come to their own doorstep.

Came midnight, and those who had stayed up for the late newscast could hardly believe their ears. The Chief-of-Staff himself was speaking:

"Soldiers of Zahal, I should like to comment briefly on the situation as it now stands. On the southern front, in the Northern Sinai sector, our forces have captured Rafah and Sheikh Zu'eid; toward evening they took El Arish. One column has gone up the El Arish–Abu-Ageila road. Other forces took Khan Yunis and Deir el Balah, and are now at the gates of Gaza.

"In the Central Sector our forces have captured Oja el-Khafir and Tarat um-Bassis, and have penetrated into the Um-Katef area. Fighting is going on there at this moment.

"In the Southern Sector, several outposts have been taken in the Kuntilla area.

"Our forces have taken many prisoners as well as much gear, including tanks and artillery.

"The enemy has suffered severe losses; ours are comparatively light.

"On the Jordanian front, the Jordanians have been shelling points all along the border and have attacked objectives from the air. The Syrian Air Force have also attacked objectives in Israeli territory.

"In the Jerusalem district, our forces have taken Zur-Bahar, the Radar Ridge and Sheikh Azziz, north of Maaleh Hakhamisha. Other forces, coming from the north, have taken several villages and are now closing in on Jenin.

"In the course of the day, the Israel Air Force dealt a decisive blow to the air forces of Egypt, Jordan and Syria, achieving air supremacy throughout the area. The Israel

HALF-TRACK COLUMN CHURNS SAND DUNES IN PURSUIT OF ENEMY.

Air Force victory of today is an unprecedented feat."

The opening day of the war was certainly Israel Air Force Day. Within *three hours* it all but wiped out the air strength of Egypt, Jordan and Syria, and left its mark on Iraq as well.

Reported IAF Commander (Brigadier-General) Mordecai Hod:

"We took on the combined air forces of Egypt, Jordan, Syria and Iraq. In this action we definitely destroyed 374 planes and perhaps 34 more. Here are the figures:

"In Egypt: 286—30 TU-16 bombers, 27 AIL-28 medium bombers, 12 of the Suchoy-7 fighter-bombers recently delivered to Egypt, 90 MIG-21's, 20 MIG-19's, 75 MIG-15's and 1 MIG-17, 32 transports and helicopters. Of all these, 20 were shot down in air action.

"In Syria: 52—30 MIG-21's, 20 MIG-17's, 2 AIL-28 bombers. In Jordan—20 Hunters and 7 transports and helicopters. In Iraq, after a wing of Iraqi planes had attacked Israeli settlements, we bombed their 3-H airfield and destroyed 6 MIG-21's and 3 Hunters.

"In this action we lost 19 men, of whom 8 were killed and 11 are missing. Some have been taken prisoner. Their families have been notified.

"Our own losses came to 4 Ouragans, 4 Mysteres, 4 Super Mysteres, 2 Mirages, 1 Vautour, and 4 Fouga-Magisters."

In two hours and fifty minutes the Egyptian Air Force had been destroyed, in the skies, on airfield runways, in the Sinai Desert and along the Nile. It took the IAF another hour to deal a crushing blow to Syrian and Jordanian air strength. By the afternoon of June 5 complete air supremacy had been achieved; the skies, as airmen say, were clean.

The results were a word-for-word compliance on the part of the fliers with the message from their commander. Said General Hod:

"Urgent. From Air Force Commander

050800 to all fighting units. Members of the Israel Air Force:

"The impudent and malicious Egyptian foe has raised his hand to destroy us. The Air Force, clenched fist of Zahal, has its orders. We are taking off for battle. The third link in the chain of our struggle for independence and freedom, in the historic land of our birth, is about to be forged. The triple thread of 1948, 1956 and 1967 shall not be snapped. The spirit of Israel's warriors throughout the generations will be with us in battle—the immortal courage of Joshua bin-Nun's men, the stalwarts of David, the Maccabees, the valiant fighters in the War of Independence and the Sinai Campaign. This spirit will be our source of strength and inspiration as we engage the Egyptian foe, the threat to our security, our

DIRECT HIT SETS EGYPTIAN ARMOR AFIRE IN TANK DUEL. UNERRING MARKSMANSHIP HELPED ZAHAL'S SUCCESS.

sovereignty and our future. In his smashing defeat we shall find peace and security for ourselves, for our children and for generations yet to come. Aloft, then! After the enemy! Smite him to oblivion and destroy his fangs! Scatter him through the desert, so that Israel may forever dwell secure in its land."

IAF members who took part in the operation told the story: "In two hours (said a young Mirage lieutenant) we accomplished more than did the air forces of France and Britain in four days, eleven years ago. It's a fact."

An Ouragan pilot: "On the last night we had a good meal and fine sleep. At dawn we went up to the briefing room and heard that our land forces had been attacked, and that soon we would be going into battle.

It all sounded like another exercise. We went up—I was Number Four in the formation—and flew toward Bir Gafgafa. Above us were the Mirages, giving us cover. We arrived, banked to the left and into range. On the first pass we hit four MIG-21's. One tried to take off but didn't make it. I then hit a MY-6 helicopter. It rose a bit, then plumped down on the burning MIG's. We hit more MIG's on the second pass, and so did the flight after us, which also took care of the anti-aircraft guns; we saw their crews ducking into the trenches and firing aimlessly. After our second pass, we peeled off and headed for Abu-Sawar, half-way between the Canal and Cairo. When we reached the airfield we found that some of our boys had already been there. The field was so overcast with smoke we

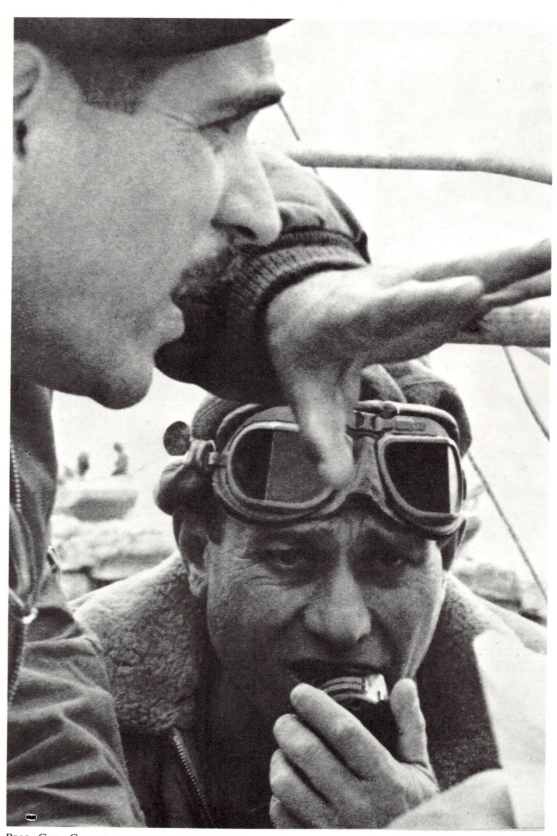

BRIG.-GEN. GAVISH, COMMANDER OF THE SOUTHERN FRONT, GIVES BATTLE ORDERS VIA INTERCOM.

couldn't find a target. The whole place was one big bonfire."

Another Ouragan pilot: "Our objective was the airfield at Fa'id, west of Bitter Lake in the Canal zone. Here we were to take care of MIG-19's, MIG-21's and Sukhoy-7's. When we arrived we found that it had already been raked pretty well by the flight that preceded ours. Bonfires all over the field marked the spot where the planes, of blessed memory, had once been. We therefore let go with our bombs and rockets and finished off everything above the surface. If any of our planes came after we did, they must have been even more disappointed than we."

A Super-Mystere pilot: "When we reached Kabrit Airfield, all the planes on the ground were already on fire. We set the hangars ablaze. On the way back we saw a freight train and asked for permission to go after it. When the permission did not come through, we bombed a few oil storage tanks. They made giant torches."

A young lieutenant: "We flew to Bardaka Airfield, south of Sharm-a-Sheikh. There were Egyptian ships on the water below us, but our target was the airfield. The ground fire didn't reach us. We came across a flight of MIG-19's on their way to protect the field. Each of us picked out a MIG and went after it. I got behind mine and let go a burst at 400 meters. The MIG blew apart right before my eyes."

IAF men had similar experiences on the Jordanian front. "After Jordanian Hunters had hit Natanya," said a wiry pilot, "we were sent to Amman to rip up the airfield and destroy the planes. Below us were two Hunters. I picked out one and hit its right wing with two bursts. The pilot dropped off the plane while it was going 600 miles an hour."

When the commanders compiled the score, at the end of the day, it all seemed impossible. Five Egyptian airfields had been completely destroyed; three others would not be immediately usable. Syria suffered five badly damaged airfields and Jordan two. The IAF fighters had flown one sortie after another, dropping their loads, returning to gulp down a sandwich and a cold drink, and off again. Some of them, though, did take a moment to read the prayer written by Chief Chaplain Goren: "May it be Thy will, O Lord our God and the God of our fathers, whose chariots are the clouds and who is borne on the wings of the wind, that Thou bear us aloft in safety and guide us in safety, and bring us to our destination, alive and in proper spirit, and that Thou protect us from every foe that lurks in the skies and on the earth, and from unexpected winds and all kinds of failures in takeoff and landing; and that we find grace and compassion in Thine eyes and in the eyes of all who see us. For Thou dost give compassionate heed, from the heavens, to the prayers of Thy people Israel. Blessed be the Lord, who hearkeneth unto prayer, and who will bid His messengers to protect you wherever you go." Other fliers, it was said, picked up a copy of the prayer, folded it several times and slipped it into their flying-jackets, muttering, "If it doesn't help, it won't do any harm either."

Chief-of-Staff General Rabin to IAF General Hod: "My felicitations on the achievement of the objective. You consummated the task efficiently, precisely and on praiseworthy levels. This is the fruit of many years of toil and preparation which have now shown their results."

In Sinai, on the ground, Egypt's first line was cracked and destroyed along the three routes mapped out by as many Zahal divisions. These were commanded by Brigadiers-General Yisrael Tal, Ariel Sharon and Avraham Yaffe. Each division was made up of brigades of armor, infantry and paratroopers, artillerymen, engineers and communication units and the medical corps. The supply system was such that each brigade could advance and move about for days independently of the others.

The Northern Route breakthrough was achieved by General Tal's men. They engaged the enemy in the Khan Yunis-Rafah sector, cleared a path for a tank column to burst through westward, captured Sheikh Zu'eid and the fortified positions at El Garadi, then advanced by evening to El Arish.

ZAHAL'S ADVANCE ACROSS SINAI, DURING FOUR STRAIGHT DAYS, IS WITHOUT LETUP.

Gen. Sharon's division broke through and demolished enemy positions at Um-Katef and Abu-Ageila, held by six artillery battalions and dozens of tanks.

The route set for Gen. Yaffe's division took it across quicksand-like dunes along the Rafa–El Arish line and north of the Nitzana–Abu-Ageila road. Here it closed in on the rear of the Egyptian forces at Bir Lahfan and sealed off their armor. Paratroopers attacked enemy positions in the rear, while armored units encircled the entire force.

At the Wadi Kurait Pass, the Egyptians had stationed an armored division to cut off Eilat from the Southern Negev. The Zahal division smashed it and went on to capture Kuntilla. To round up things in the north, an infantry unit cleaned up Khan Yunis, captured Deir el Balah and, after hard fighting, overran the position at Ali Mumtar at the gates of Gaza.

In the Jerusalem sector, the Zahal action began to take shape late in the afternoon. Infantry units attached to the armored brigade commanded by Col. Uri Ben-Ari moved from Maaleh Hakhamisha and, with Radar Ridge and Sheikh Abdul Azziz subdued, went on through the dusk to the heights of Nebi Samuel, opposite Jerusalem on the north. Another column, having worked its way up through Bet-Horon from captured Latrun, joined up with the units in preparation for the assault on Ramallah.

In the "Big Triangle" area held by Jordan, a diversionary move was made out of Beisan. At the same time, a major attack was directed at Jenin, the apex of the area.

The attack was launched at 3 a.m. Hard-fighting Legionnaires, handling their anti-tank guns skilfully, were strung out along the hillocks commanding the approaches to the town. The Jordanians also had Patton tanks against Zahal's Sherman models of '50 and '51. Fate seemed to hang in the balance as sixty new Pattons came up, but before they could get into position they were raked mercilessly by anti-tank

◄ ONE BATTLE OVER, ANOTHER LOOMS AHEAD. ZAHAL UNITS RE-GROUP FOR NEXT OBJECTIVE.

His truck hopelessly imbedded in the sand, Egyptian soldier decides to call the whole thing off.

NAVAL UNITS BROUGHT THE WAR TO ENEMY PORTS.

and aircraft fire, followed immediately by a surge of Zahal infantry. Jenin fell and whoever of the Legionnaires was left was in flight.

Such was the balance sheet for June 5, 1967, the first day of the war. Who had started the actual fighting? Opinions naturally varied, but none vacillated as strangely as Reuters. Early in the morning Reuters had flashed the news to the world: "Egypt has launched an attack on Israel." By 9:50 Reuters had undergone a change of heart and asked its clients throughout the world to make a slight correction, namely, "Israel has launched an attack against Egypt." But then, everyone is entitled to make a mistake once in a while.

And speaking about the sources of information for the press, some words should be devoted to the hundreds of foreign correspondents, representing individual newspapers in all corners of the globe as well as reporters for the wire services, the radio and television professionals who came to the Middle East to tell the story of a conflict and found there material which gave their by-lines the greatest reading and listening excitement of the century.

They did a masterful job. If the television staffs are to be singled out, it is because this medium did more to tell the story of the war than any other medium could possibly have done. Many an Israeli later received enthused reports from friends and relatives abroad on the outstanding series of telecasts which emanated from the battlefields of Sinai and other theaters of operation. The Israelis, with only educational television in operation at the present, could only be happy that the story—*their* story— was reaching the peoples of the free world.

The entire coverage of the war, between Israel and those who sought to destroy it, is a credit to the Fourth Estate. Members of the profession risked—and three of them lost—their lives on the fast-moving fronts, in quest of the true picture of events, on the outcome of which much of the world's future was hanging in the balance.

# FROM LATRUN TO GAZA

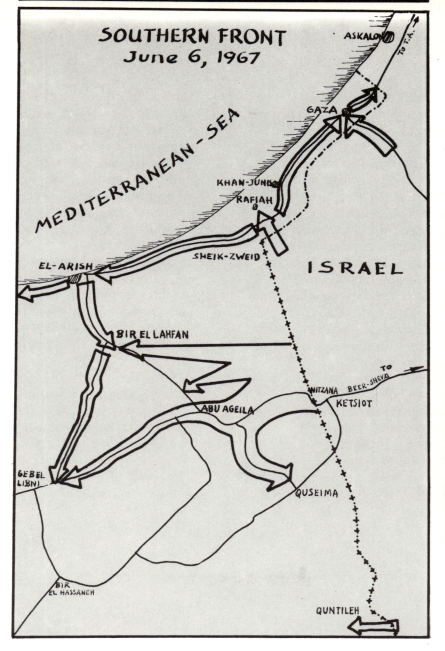

SOUTHERN FRONT
June 6, 1967

MEDITERRANEAN - SEA

ASKALON

TO T.A.

GAZA

KHAN-JUNIS

RAFIAH

SHEIK-ZWEID

ISRAEL

EL-ARISH

BIR EL LAHFAN

TO
BEER-SHEVA

NITZANA

KETSIOT

ABU AGEILA

GEBEL
LIBNI

QUSEIMA

BIR
EL HASSANEH

QUNTILEH

WRECKAGE OF EGYPTIAN ARMOR BLOCKS ROAD TO GAZA.

THE story of the second day of the war was written chiefly by Zahal armor.

Toward nightfall on the previous day, Zahal's Pattons, Centurions, AMX's and half-tracks had advanced well toward El Arish, only to find the re-grouped Egyptian forces entrenched at El Garadi, just to the north of it. A night attack had to be launched with armor and infantry in order to clear the path to El Arish for the entire division.

The going was slow and difficult. The attackers were met by heavy rifle, machine-gun and mortar fire from the surrounding sand dunes. Furthermore, the Egyptians had mined the entire area, and brilliant flares dispelled the advantages of darkness. Finally all resistance had been overcome, and the entire division moved on to El Arish.

(In the course of the battle, four paratroopers captured an Egyptian jeep laden with bottles of brandy and Coca-Cola. They smeared the vehicle fondly with sand and grease and dragged it off, thus camouflaged, as "an appended vehicle".)

From El Arish the division advanced in two columns. One force headed west, toward the Suez Canal. The other encircled the important airfield of the town. The field was strewn with the smoking remains of

EGYPTIANS ABANDON CARS IN FLIGHT.

IN GAZA'S POLICE STATION, ZAHAL SOLDIERS HAVE FIRST GOOD REST IN MANY HOURS.

ZAHAL HALF-TRACKS ROLL THROUGH GAZA IN SEARCH OF SNIPERS' NESTS.

A PROUD MOMENT FOR POSTERITY—A MEMENTO OF "IN THOSE DAYS".

MAJ.-GENERAL ABDUL MUN'AM HUSSEINI SIGNS SURRENDER PAPERS.

MIG's, targets of IAF bull's-eye bombing. On the polished tables in the ornate officers' dining room, the beer mugs stood half-filled; the officers had departed, leaving the foot-soldiers huddled in the hangars, half-dead with thirst.

"These are the soldiers whom you were expecting to capture Israel?" a Zahal officers' dining room, the beer mugs stood escape in time.

"What do you want of me?" returns the Egyptian, in polished English. "Ask them who sent us to fight this bloody war."

Prisoners are being taken by the hundreds all along the line. Near Sheikh-Zu'eid, a truckload of Egyptian soldiers wanders in from the darkness, smack into the Zahal encampment. "Welcome, O reinforcements from Iraq!" cries the driver, his eyes bleary with sand and sweat. Eventually he and his passengers discover the error.

An Egyptian command post between El Arish and Abu-Ageila yields, besides prisoners, several Hebrew-language pamphlets, evidently part of the material supplied by Nasser's education office to prepare Egyptian officers for Tel-Aviv. The pamphlets contain a hodge-podge of quotations, slang, aphorisms, and such handy phrases as "I love you! Please remain faithful to me!"

The fighting goes on. Units of General Yaffe's division catch up with fleeing

ZAHAL UNIT ENJOYS THE SERENITY OF GAZA UNDER ▶ JRFEW.

LOOKOUT POINT ATOP HOTEL AMBASSADOR HELPS SPOT SNIPERS.

WALLS, WINDOWS IN JERUSALEM
HIT BY SHELLS.

ZAHAL SHARPSHOOTERS EXCHANGE SHOTS WITH SNIPERS IN AMERICAN COLONY.

Egyptian tanks, halt them for good, then join up with General Tal's division for action west and south. In the meantime, General Sharon's division continues the breakthrough at Um-Katef and heads toward Quseima.

The hour of Gaza has come. Zahal infantry units, joined by paratroopers and supported by tanks, capture Gaza in a bloody battle. The Strip is in Israeli hands.

Advancing through the ancient Philistine city, Zahal soldiers find, in the basement of the hospital, a high-ranking officer surrounded by ten others. It turns out that the gentleman is Major-General Abdul Mun'im Husseini, Military Governor of Gaza and commander of all the Egyptian forces in the area. At first he claims that he is making the rounds of the wards, but it is quickly discovered (there being no patients in the building with the Red Crescent flying above it) that the hospital was being used by the Egyptians as staff headquarters. Gen. Husseini calmly tells his captors that this is his third encounter with Zahal. He was a member of Kaukgi's "Liberation Army" in 1948 and a lieutenant in the Sinai Campaign. He does not seem to be in the least disturbed by his having been taken captive.

Jerusalem remains pinned down in its shelters by indiscriminate Jordanian shelling, now in its second day. The streets are deserted, except for civil defense workers darting from building to building. The shelling reaches Hadassah Hospital, but the surgeons in the emergency operating room continue with their brain operations. Five births are placed on the books, and, in the Hospital shelters, there are three circumcisions.

In the outlying suburbs north of the Old City, the battle is raging with awful intensity. Col. Ben-Ari's brigade is battling to control the Ramallah area, the key to the entire West Bank. His tanks and half-tracks do impossible twists and turns on the rocky slopes, again and again catching the enemy by surprise. Sheikh-Jarah falls, then French Hill and the Rockefeller Museum. Two battalions are dispatched

ZAHAL WARRIOR FINDS UNIQUE PROP FOR PRAYING.

ZAHAL TAKES AIRPORT AT ATAROT, LOST IN 1948 WAR.

ADVANCE OF ZAHAL ARMOR ALONG SEEMINGLY IMPREGNABLE ROCKY HILLSIDES CAUGHT JORDANIANS BY SURPRISE.

Jerusalem environs and names to remember: Police Academy, Victoria Augusta, Abu-Tor.

SINAI ON THE SECOND DAY OF THE WAR.

ZAHAL NULLIFIES EGYPT'S TEN-YEAR INVESTMENT IN ARMOR, MEN AND MATERIALS.

EGYPTIAN RESISTANCE BROKEN, ZAHAL VEHICLES ROLL THROUGH SINAI.

Spoils, 1967 style: A smiling bigger-than-life portrait of Nasser

to take Ramallah. Along the way they pass Neve Yaaqov and Atarot, two settlements which Israel had been forced to abandon in 1948.

Latrun, the infamous fortress half-way between Tel-Aviv and Jerusalem, falls after a two-hour battle. Zahal enters the town. To the right is the monastery of the Trappist Order; to the left, the huge police fortress. Below is the town, totally abandoned. In a nearby field are the ruins of houses, broken concrete pillars, twisted and rusty tin roofs, broken doors, jagged windows. This is where the British Mandatory regime had incarcerated the heads of the Jewish community in Palestine on the "Black Sabbath" of 1947, in an attempt to wrest from them the secrets of the Jewish underground. The broken-up Latrun highway, weeds growing through its cracked surface, is now open to Israeli vehicles.

As the Zahal units move off to the east, an Egyptian commando unit, air-lifted from Amman two days earlier, attempts an ambush. The Egyptians are wiped out.

Ramallah surrenders. The forces of the Northern Command now put heavy pressure toward the south, while from the west, infantry units converge on Qalqilya and reach Azun. About noon an armored brigade captures Jenin. And once again history repeats itself: The brigade commander to whom had been assigned the task of taking Jenin is the same young company commander who had taken the town nineteen years and five days earlier, when his armored column had burst into the town, held it until midnight, then was forced to withdraw when Iraqi units, supported by artillery and tanks, launched a counterattack. Then, nineteen years earlier, the fortified police building had not been captured. This time the commander, a member of Kibbutz Hotrim, began where Company 21 could not go on in 1948; the first objective in Jenin was the police building. Mayor Husseini Suky, dressed in his Friday best, now presents himself before the commander, asks that the residents of the town not be harmed, and promises full

PART OF ABANDONED BOOTY.

VERY FIRST DAY REVEALED EXTENT

OF ARMOR ABANDONED BY EGYPTIANS.

A TESTIMONIAL TO IAF MARKSMANSHIP.

◄ NEW TANKS CAPTURED IN THEIR PITS.

cooperation. Then he adds: "On the first of June in 1948 I was going to submit a surrender petition to the commander of the Israeli forces who had taken the town. When I arose in the morning and went to the Municipal Building I saw that they had disappeared, as though the earth had swallowed them."

Suddenly, at the Kabatya crossroads, the Zahal forces run into Jordanian troops. The skirmish is brief, and the Israelis arrive in the vicinity of Nablus in time to join other units driving on the town. Here the tank duel lasts until midnight; part of the Zahal armor is dispatched to Damia Bridge to block possible Jordanian reinforcements from the East Bank.

Repercussions from abroad will also be making the next morning's headlines . . . Cyprus President Archbishop Makarios has taken a pro-Arab stand in the conflict; his note to Nasser brands Israel as the aggressor . . . British Prime Minister Wilson announces a 24-hour embargo on arms shipments to the Middle East, pending talks with the Kremlin on the new state of affairs . . . Holland announces that arms shipments to Israel—radar equipment, light anti-aircraft guns, spare parts for planes and jeeps—are continuing, in accordance with an agreement previously reached by the two countries . . . Danish Prime Minister Kampmann inaugurates a

MANY PRISONERS TOOK THE PRECAUTION TO CHANGE INTO CIVVIES.

national campaign to aid Israel . . . In India, Mrs. Ghandi accuses Israel of having connived the Middle East war . . . Yugoslavia places itself at the side of the "justified struggle" being waged by the Arabs . . . Turkey, Japan and Thailand make public their perfect neutrality . . . The UN Security Council, having listened to Israel's delegate Gideon Rafael and Egypt's delegate Muhammed Awad el-Kouny, adjourns for deliberations.

Back in Jerusalem, Zahal is re-grouping for the decisive battle. Its Jerusalem Brigade has taken Abu-Tor, east of the railway station, after a long battle. In the conquered areas around the City, units are engaged in final mopping-up operations. The morrow has been set aside by history for the Battle for Jerusalem.

MARSHAL AMER IS IN FAMILY PICTURE.

ISRAEL'S COLORS GO UP—AN OFT-
REPEATED SCENE IN THE WAR.
THIS ONE IS AT EL ARISH.

76

No borders—no incidents. A position at this border kibbutz can now relax.

PAUSING AT A SINAI CROSSROADS, BOYS HAVE A BITE AND A SMOKE.

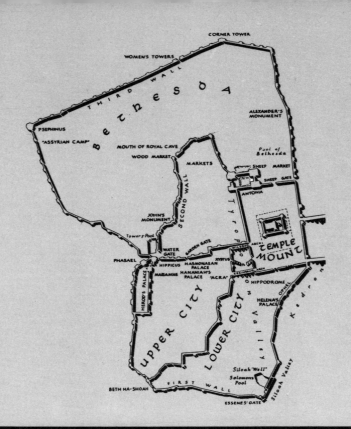

# TEMPLE MT.—TIRAN DAY

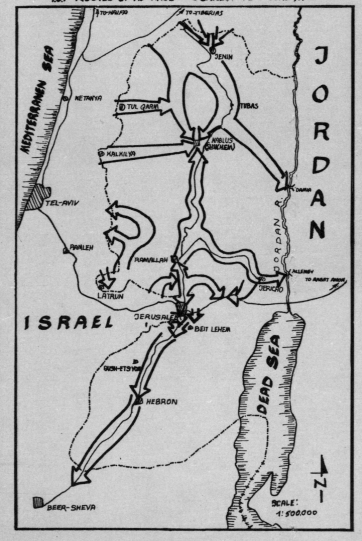

I.D.F. ROUTES OF ADVANCE — CORRECT TO 7 JUNE, 1967

A UNIT RETURNS FIRE DURING FIRST TOUGH MOMENTS IN BATTLE FOR JERUSALEM.

FROM the Mount of Olives, Col. Mordecai ("Mota") Gur issued, in the early hours of the morning, the following orders:

"Attention all Brigade Commanders:

"We are now positioned on a ridge overlooking the Old City. Soon we shall be inside it—the ancient City of Jerusalem, the hope and dream of many generations. This is our objective: the Paratroop Brigade is to capture the Old City and the Temple Mount; tanks will proceed through Lions Gate; First and Second Battalions will go there at once. The Third Battalion will leave a small force on the ridge and also move to the Gate. At the close of this operation, a brigade review will be held on Temple Mount Square.

"Paratroopers, on to Jerusalem! That is all."

*Khativon*, the Paratroop Brigade newspaper, later published these excerpts from the Col.'s notebook, jotted down in the command half-track:

"I opened the door-hatch. Below was the Old City—glorious, impressive . . . At last, our Jerusalem . . . Below, Jordanian soldiers in flight. One tank burning . . . Azaria Village on the right, Lassad below. Pass tanks, enter Abu-Dis. Halt tanks at Zecharia crossroads . . . Am returning to Hilton Hotel entrance. The Old City is below us; we shall be taking it soon . . . Halt the artillery; I want to see what's going on (First Battalion gets orders to prepare to move; Second Battalion gets orders to prepare for action) . . . Artillery, fire! . . . Tanks, forward! . . . Abu-Dis Ridge is ours . . . The first tank is at Lions Gate. We are driving to the Old City. Tanks are almost inside, guns blazing. Halt the artillery. We go inside. I urge Etan on, pass him and drive to the advance tanks to urge them on . . . We are halted by a

ments imaginable—to break through a built-up, easily defended area. This demanded top-level fighting on the part of every man. Here one can't take sights at a distance or compute a course. Here all you can do is give an order; the boys must then take over and carry on to the end of the operation. Our objectives were put to us in general terms. We were to reach Mount Scopus, then pave the way for an assault on the Old City. *The Old City*—those words lit up the go-ahead green light in our hearts.

"The fighting around Jerusalem was already thick and heavy. The sector from which we were to make our move was under unremitting enemy fire. I realized with some chagrin that my officers weren't as familiar with the terrain as I had hoped they'd be. We therefore had to call on the Jerusalem Brigade to help us out in the initial stages. Our headquarters were set up in one of the buildings.

"At nightfall, the unit commanders went up to the border for a look at the enemy positions. We held a final briefing, scanned maps of the area and prepared to move.

"We had hoped to launch the attack at midnight, but were held up because of the intricate pattern of the buildings in the area. It took some time to map out the evacuation routes, for we knew that we would be suffering many casualties in wounded men.

"It was one o'clock in the morning. Now the question arose whether it might not be better to wait until morning and move under air cover. The unit commanders, however, preferred to cross over from New Jerusalem into the fortified Jordanian area under cover of darkness. At 2:20 a.m. it was finally decided to move. The brigade command went up to the roof to direct the action.

"The firing became worse as soon as we began setting off our explosive charges. Since the enemy had the entire area in his sights, our casualties began even before we could make contact with the Jordanians. The wounded were beside themselves. 'Hell, we didn't even get to fire a shot or throw a grenade. What kind of war is this?'

burning tank. Drive past it. Haim Bar-Lev spoke to me. We are at the Gate. Burning vehicle ahead. We proceed slowly . . . We are inside! We are inside! The Temple Mount is ours! Moishe'le is on his way to plant the flag on the Western Wall!"
The full account of the operation, which is already a chapter by itself in Jewish history, was told a few days later by Col. "Mota":
"When the war broke out on Monday, we were at an airfield, ready for a parajump. A paratrooper's highest ambition is to do a parajump in actual combat. All of us were excited about the prospect. The battalions were all over the field.

"About 2 p.m., we received orders to get one battalion to Jerusalem. I went to check with the Brigadier and found that two battalions would be going. By the time I returned, the entire brigade had been ordered out. By this time we knew that we were to take on one of the toughest assign-

"We brought up our artillery. Our tanks came down the streets and took up positions. The shelling grew heavier. One shell hit our building, and the flying stones barely missed our communications men. The tanks, manned by Jerusalemites, moved forward quickly, cracking the enemy positions. Behind them the battalions fanned out, one toward the Police Academy and the other toward Sheikh-Jerrah.

"I have gone through many battles, but the stories I heard from my officers about this one are beyond belief. The fighting moved from one post to another, along trenches, around boulders. One company made it with only four men left. Another, by the time it captured the southern tip of Sheikh-Jerrah, had only seven. They had to break through five stone fences and cross open territory before they reached enemy trenches, and these were bristling with men and weapons.

"Two companies—Dadi's and Dudik's—charged toward the trenches. Here there was no possibility of a flanking attack; at some point a direct attack had to be made on a bunker. The Jordanians had constructed these tier upon tier. Their command headquarters was in a deep cellar—very cool and comfortable—which was part of a long cave with many exits, somewhat like the caves in Sanhedria. Most of the bunkers were of concrete. Later we went back to examine these positions to see the results of our artillery fire, which we found to have been amazingly accurate. Several bunkers had received direct hits and were shattered, while others which had been hit point blank were hardly nicked.

"The fighting was now hand-to-hand, from house to house, in cellars, on top of roofs. Every house on their side had been turned into a fortress. It took us four hours to clean them out. The commanders were in the lead and the men were right behind them. They came up to a bunker, connected to the trench. Two heavy machine-guns were firing out of it. One of our soldiers, David Shalom, climbed on top of it and threw in a grenade. It went off, but the firing went on. Someone threw him three explosive charges. These, too, went

off, killing some of the Jordanians, but the others kept on firing. Shalom then crept in through the trench and silenced the bunker with a second grenade.

"There were many other soldiers who displayed astounding courage. A young fellow by the name of Naftali, who was standing guard against attack on the flank of the unit, pivoted about and ran up and down the trenches around him, firing as he went, until he was wounded. Now he is doing fine.

"There were many such instances. Our boys kept going back and forth for ammunition and replacements. The unit commanders kept sending back the same report: 'Give us a little more time and everything will be under control. Just get the wounded out of here.'

"I want to mention the work of the medics. Based on what the men have already told me, I am recommending seven of them for citations. Nir, second in command of his company, was running along a trench when he caught sight of one of his machine-gunners, wounded but unaware of it. Finally, he said to Nir: 'What've I got?' Nir looked and saw a hole in the man's thigh. He put his finger into the hole to stop the blood and yelled for a medic. One suddenly appeared, took hold of the gunner and motioned Nir to go on. I later learned that he was our last medic, and he was taking care of all the wounded.

"Then there was the nurse who came with the ambulance. When she found that all the doctors had been wounded, she refused to leave and stayed with the brigade all the time.

"At daybreak, we brought in the tanks. They fanned out over the area and worked over one house after another, up to the Rockefeller Museum. At the same time, the Third Battalion was brought in from Mandelbaum Gate toward Herod's Gate, where the infantry was to make its break-

OPPOSITE: PARATROOPERS PREPARE TO STORM THE ▶ OLD CITY.

NEXT THREE PHOTOS: PARATROOPER UNIT ADVANCES UNDER HEAVY FIRE AS IT STRIKES INTO OLD CITY; ▶ TAKES COVER AGAINST SNIPERS; ARAB LEGIONNAIRES SURRENDER.

through into the Old City. When I joined the Battalion later in the morning, at the Rivoli Hotel, I found its commander there with only seventeen men, two of them wounded. The others were scattered throughout the area, fighting on their own. I knew they had suffered many casualties, since their advance had been along the main streets of the suburbs.

"Our Engineers Corps had been working in the Police Academy area for four hours, under heavy fire, to clear a path for the tanks. We still had to take the Augusta Victoria ridge overlooking the Old City, where Jordanian artillery commanded our approach to it. Time was now of the essence. I dispatched a battalion to Mount Scopus to make an assault on Augusta Victoria via the highway connecting the two hills; this approach would undoubtedly be watched by the enemy, but we had no choice. Another battalion would execute a frontal attack by coming up the slope from below; this, too, was risky, since its back would be to the Old City walls, but I had to chance it. The third battalion would move in the shadow of the walls, despite the fire from above, and attempt to get to the Temple Mount.

"At 8:30 a.m., the air bombardment began. Our tanks advanced under its cover, firing

ZAHAL MEDIC SNIPS AWAY UNIFORM FROM CHEST OF WOUNDED SOLDIER.

Wounded comrade is carried back under fire to evacuation area.

VIA DOLOROSA

طريق الآلام

A LOOK UP
VIA DOLOROSA.

PARATROOPER UNIT MOVES TOWARD LIONS GATE. HERE ATTACK WAS LAUNCHED ON TEMPLE MOUNT.

steadily. Then all action went into high gear. The battalion on Mount Scopus moved quickly up the road and, at the same time, the frontal attack was launched from below. Knowing that the ridge was well-fortified, we kept raking it with artillery fire. The Jordanians were now on the run, looking for places to hide. Our half-track reached the hotel atop the next ridge. We stopped for a moment on the terrace. Below us was the Old City, its domes—one gold, the other silver—glistening in the morning sun. Beyond lay the New Jerusalem. I gave the battalions the order to advance and offered congratulations to the one who would get into the Old City first.

"We saturated the Old City with artillery fire, around the area of Herod's Gate, where we could expect the heaviest resistance. We kept the shells close to the top of the walls so as not to hit any of the holy places. The heaviest fire was directed at the breakthrough point.

"When we saw the tanks advancing, we caught up with them and ordered greater speed. At the moat bridge near Lions Gate the maneuvering became complicated, but our tanks just kept on going.

"Our driver was a bearded fellow by the name of Ben-Zur. He tended to move along calmly, but when I told him 'Drive on!' he drove on. Near the gate a vehicle was burning, all but barring the way. But Ben-Zur had his orders, and he zoomed past it. At the gate a door swung, half-open; no doubt there were grenades above it. Ben-Zur sent the half-track right through, taking the door with him and just missing the shower of stones that came toppling down. An Arab was standing off to one side; would he be letting go with a grenade? Ben-Zur didn't give him time to make up his mind, but sped right by. We turned left to the third gate. It was open, but a motorcycle straddled the entrance; mined, no doubt, we thought. But Ben-Zur had his orders. He flattened the motorcycle (it had not been mined) and a moment later

◄ A WEARY WARRIOR AND HIS NECKLACE.

WOUNDED IN THE APPROACH TO THE WESTERN WALL.

he halted the half-track on the Temple Mount.

"Our assignment had been carried out. There was to be no more firing, not in the sacred area. The Jordanians had not shelled it, either. At this point the tanks could go no farther, and the infantry prepared to take over.

"The mayor of the Old City and the Kadi now came up and told me that the citizenry had decided not to resist. The Jordanian army was gone. I agreed to refrain from shooting as long as we were not shot at. The mayor said he could not be responsible for the snipers. In general we met no opposition, although we lost four men in the process.

"When it was all over, we had one battalion stationed at Nablus Gate, another atop the wall overlooking Yemin Moshe, and a third at Dung Gate adjoining Mount Zion. Our position, I might say, was not bad at all.

"And who were these men of the Brigade which took Jerusalem?

"They were, indeed, the cream of the crop. Many had taken part in reprisal actions, over the years. Some had been wounded but came back. They had been in the Sinai Campaign, passed active service age for paratroopers, and were highly indignant when they received their discharge papers.

UNIT COMMANDER CHECKS HIS ORDERS DURING LULL IN JERUSALEM FIGHTING.

LIFE, DEATH AND COUNTING
BEADS GO ON.

ALREADY INSIDE OLD CITY, WEARY SOLDIERS STILL HAD TO CHECK FOR SNIPERS.

FIRST PRAYERS AT THE WALL. SCROLL OF LAW, BROUGHT BY CHIEF CHAPLAIN, NESTLES IN NICHE OF SACRED STONES.

All of them signed special applications for further service with some paratroop unit.

"We saw them now, in the hospitals. They grabbed our hands and made us give them two promises: first, to capture the Syrian highlands. There they were—hardly able to move or even breathe, yet all that concerned them was the Syrian campaign. Secondly, they wanted to be back with the Brigade as soon as they got out. You ask yourself: What motivates these people? Where do they get this courage, this self-reliance? And can any commander really be worthy to have such men with him—men who undertake any responsibility in the stress of battle—men who make decisions, take the initiative. If they see the situation calls for a tank, they run back and bring a tank.

"And mind you, these are not battle-tried men. Many had not previously taken part in a single engagement. More than that—paratroopers are not trained for action in a built-up area; this is a job for regular infantry. But you should have seen how quickly they adapted themselves to the situation, to weapons they had never seen before. How they attacked! How they bound up the wounds of others! These are MEN!"

The Third Day, 10:05 a.m.—A paratrooper of the lead group which had broken through Lions Gate runs headlong through the dark, crooked alleys. At the turn in the alley he stops dead in his tracks:

"Fellows, the Wall! I see the Wall! The Western Wall!" The others come pouring into the enclosure—tough paratroopers, red-eyed and caked with dust, chins scraggy with hair turned to wire by blood, they now kneel by the huge ancient stones, press their blackened fingers into the crevices, weeping like children. A broad-shouldered paratrooper keeps running about, screaming like a madman: "Jerusalem is ours! Jerusalem is ours!"

At 10:15, the Star of David is unfurled over the Temple Mount. The Western Wall gets a misty-eyed honor guard. A Zahal unit fires a proud volley. Paratroopers hug each other. The unit commander reports to the Brigadier: "The Temple Mount is in my hands! I repeat—the Temple Mount is in my hands!"

An imposing, fiery figure appears on the scene—the Chief Chaplain of Zahal, Brig.-Gen. Shlomo Goren. In one hand he is holding a small Scroll of the Law in a purple coverlet. With the other he whips out a ram's horn, raises it to his lips, and a blast rolls like thunder through the enclosure. "These moments," cries the Chief Chaplain, "will be inscribed in the annals of our people for generations to come! Zahal has raised the flag of Israel's sovereignty over the Temple Mount, site of the nation's glory!" He hardly pauses for breath. "The Wall is ours! We shall never give it up!"

A few minutes later come the C-o-S,

PARATROOPERS ENTER AREA WHERE THE TEMPLE HAD ONCE STOOD.

Gen. Rabin; the Assistant C-o-S, Brig.-Gen. Haim Barlev; Brig.-Gen. Uzzi Narkiss, head of the Central Command; senior officers and the soldiers who achieved the breakthrough. They all join in an inspired Mincha (vesper) service.

And this is the proclamation issued by the Chief Chaplain in honor of the day:

Fighting men of Israel, beloved of the nation, crowned with valorous victory.

The Lord be with you, stalwarts of the host!

I am addressing you from the court of the Western Wall, remnant of our Temple.

Comfort ye, comfort ye my people, said you Lord.

This is the day for which we have longed, let us be glad and rejoice in its salvation.

The vision of all the generations has come to pass before our eyes. The City of God, the site of the Temple, the Temple Mount and the Western Wall, symbol of the Messianic redemption of our people, have this day been redeemed by you, valorous men of Zahal. Today you have made good the oath of generations: "If I forget thee, O Jerusalem, so let my right hand be forgotten." And indeed, we have not forgotten thee, O Jerusalem, our sacred city and home of our glory, and our right hand —the right hand of God—has wrought this historic redemption.

Whose heart will fail to sing and resound at the news of this redemption! Now there will be opened the gates of Zion and of ancient Jerusalem. The paths to the Western Wall will be open to the prayers of its sons and liberators, here, and of the Jewish people everywhere, as they ascend to make their supplications before the Creator.

The Divine Spirit, which has never detached itself from the Western Wall, now goes forth before the hosts of Israel in a pillar of fire, illuminating for us the road to victory and surrounding us with clouds of honor, before all men.

Happy are we who have earned this noblest hour in the history of our People!

And to the nations of the world we say: We shall protect, with dignity and with honor, all the sites sanctified to all people of peace and trust, and their gates will be open wide to men of all faiths.

Dear sons and soldiers! Through you the nation has achieved this highest of privileges. The prayers of generations and the visions of the prophets have come to life: "For Thou, O Lord, didst set it afire, and with fire willst Thou build it, as it is said: 'And I shall be unto her, saith the Lord, an encircling wall of fire, and within her I shall be honored.' Blessed be Thou, O Lord, comforter of Zion and builder of Jerusalem."

And to Zion and the remnant of our Temple we bring these tidings: The sons have returned to within their boundaries. Our feet are now standing in thy gates, O Jerusalem, the City now joined together

WORN-OUT CONQUERORS OF JERUSALEM ENJOY BELATED LUNCH.

ROUGH-HEWN VICTOR IN HUMBLE PRAYER AT THE WALL.

DOWN TO THE
WESTERN WALL.

C-o-S Gen. Rabin, Defense Minister Gen. Dayan and Brig.-Gen. Narkiss enter Old City via Lions Gate.

Chief Chaplain Brig.-Gen. Goren sounds ram's horn at Wall, moments after its liberation. ▶

THE FLAG OF ISRAEL FLIES ABOVE OLD CITY WALLS.

JORDANIAN PLANS TO CAPTURE NEW JERUSALEM.

with the new Jewish Jerusalem, the City beautiful, joy of all the land, capital of eternal Israel.

In the name of the communities of Israel, here and in the Diaspora, I pronounce, with supreme joy, the Benediction: 'Blessed be Thou, O Lord our God, King of the universe, for having given us life, fulfillment, and the attainment of this moment.'

This year—in Jerusalem Rebuilt!

Half-tracks roll up with other guests: Rabbi Zvi Yehuda Kook, son of Chief Rabbi Kook, of blessed memory; Rabbi David Cohen and his son, Rabbi Shear-Yishuv Cohen, now Vice-Mayor of Jerusalem, who, as the last soldier to leave Old Jerusalem in 1948, had once been the prisoner of the Jordanians. All pronounce the Benediction and join in a dance of gratitude and praise to the Almighty.

It does not take long before congratulatory messages inundate the "Bet Hannasee", official residence of President Zalman Shazar of Israel, who had just returned from an abbreviated visit abroad. They come from highly-placed statesmen and farmers, from mayors of cities around the globe, from Israeli fishing smacks ("We are doing fine, but Zahal caught the biggest") and a farm organization deep in Colombia. "We get it coming and going," complained good-naturedly a Ministry of Posts official. "When it looked like war would break out, we had our hands full with cables from

Zahal soldiers on Temple Mount. Background: Dome of the Rock.

Next page: The Western Wall greets its liberators.

JORDAN VALLEY, JERICHO UNFOLD BEFORE EYES OF ADVANCING ZAHAL UNITS.

"WELCOME TO BETHLEHEM" SIGN; NOT ORIGINALLY INTENDED FOR ZAHAL.

SOLDIERS ATOP MT. GERIZIM, SITE SACRED TO THE SAMARITANS.

Zahal armor takes West Bank's three key towns: Nablus (Shechem), Ramallah, Jericho.

114

Soldiers at famous Ramallah radio station.

Damia Bridge, destroyed during "Night of Bridges" in 1946.

WEST BANK ARABS WHO DECIDED TO LEAVE TAKE JERICHO ROAD TO AMMAN.

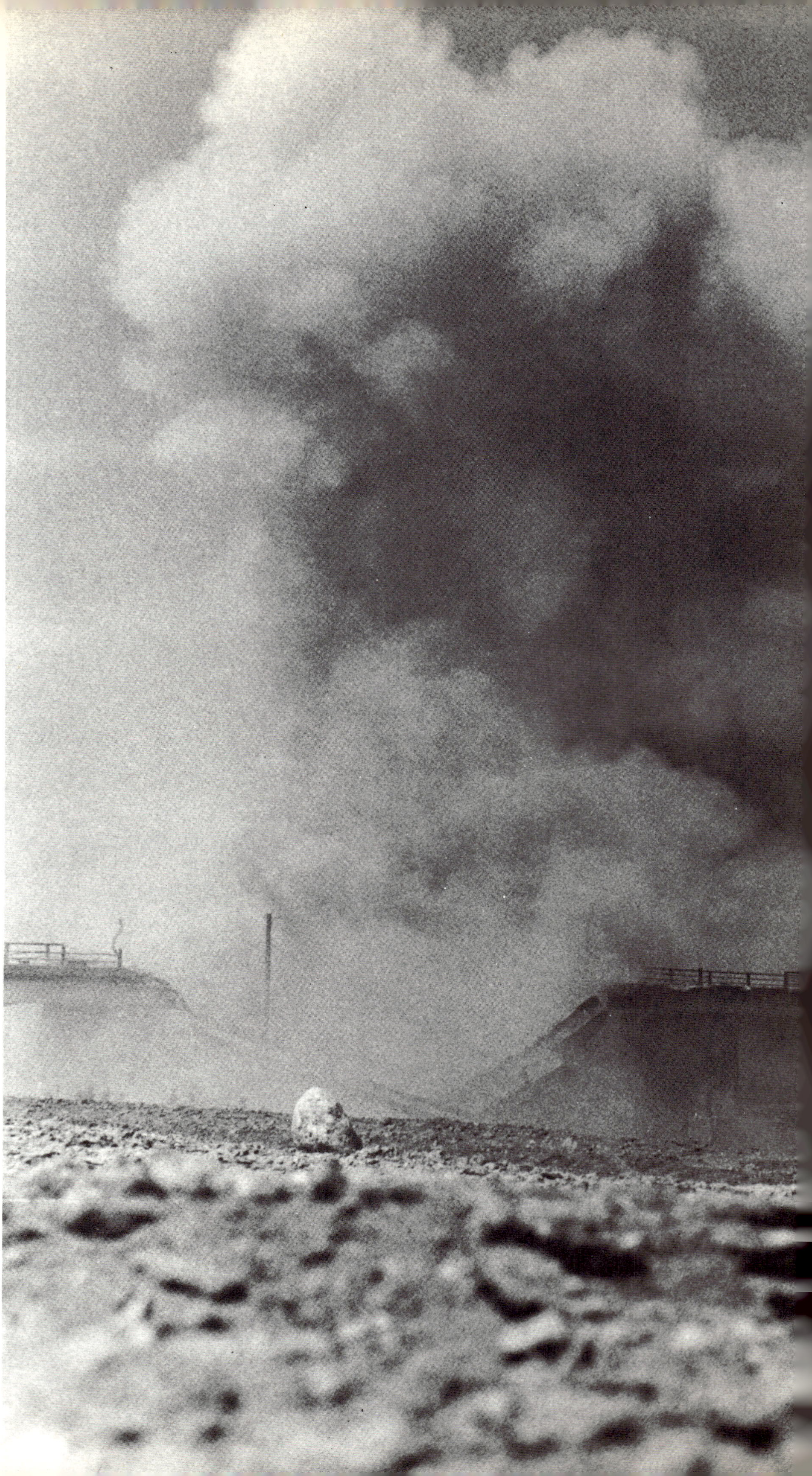

COL. URI BEN-ARI AND HIS ARMORED BRIGADE, WHICH CAPTURED MOST OF THE WEST BANK.

◄ ALLENBY BRIDGE, LARGEST SPANNING THE JORDAN, IN COLLAPSE.

abroad to relatives and friends here. But that was nothing compared with the number coming in now."

It is a great day especially for two Zahal commanders: the second-in-command of the Palmach Fourth Battalion, who broke through into the Old City in 1948 but was forced to give it up—Gen. Uzzi Narkiss, whose forces now liberated the Temple Mount. The other, commander of the Fourth Battalion in 1948 and now the C-o-S of Zahal, Gen. Itzhak Rabin.

The sounds of firing and explosions are still all around. Zahal units are clearing away snipers' nests and mine fields.

Shell-riddled Jerusalem, cramped from three days of shelters but quiet and courageous, is emotionally overwhelmed but exceedingly glad of heart. Everyone surges toward the Western Wall, to see it, to touch its stones. Pious Jews risk the

mine fields and infiltrate past the guards to reach the Wall, by devious short-cuts, for a moment of fervent prayer, as if to make up for the years of forced separation.

Defense Minister Moshe Dayan visits the Wall: "Zahal has this morning reunited the division of Jerusalem, the amputated capital of Israel. We have returned to the holiest of our sites; we have returned and shall never again be separated from it." He then inserts a bit of paper into a crevice, in the old tradition.

Prime Minister Levi Eshkol is jubilant yet humble: "I regard myself as the emissary of the entire people, as the emissary of so many generations of our people, whose souls yearned for Jerusalem and its sanctity."

David Ben-Gurion's voice rings out: "This is a great day for the entire Jewish People! There are no words to describe the debt which the Jewish People owes to valorous Zahal!''

Units continue to comb the alleys, house after house. Many of the Arab men seem to have just gotten up, since they are still wearing pyjamas—but beneath many pyjamas are Jordan Legion uniforms . . .

News of the events in Jerusalem are broadcast to the country. At an air base far from the Western Wall the following took place:

When Private Yossef Hudida, now 30, reached Bar Mitzva age, he did not observe the tradition of donning phylacteries because he was then living in an unfriendly Arab country. Now, with all of Jerusalem and the Western Wall in Israel's possession, Yossef Hudida came to a conclusion: God has not abandoned His People; he, Yossef Hudida, will not abandon God. He went to the encampment synagogue, put on phylacteries, said his prayers, and addressed his comrades on the importance of the occasion. Yossef Hudida became Bar Mitzvah—at 30.

Zahal now leaves the rejoicing to the populace and surges onward. A tank column under Col. Uri Ben-Ari rumbles through Ramallah, fires a few warning shots—white flags are fluttering everywhere—and goes on to Jericho. Several soldiers, aware of their destination, and with no

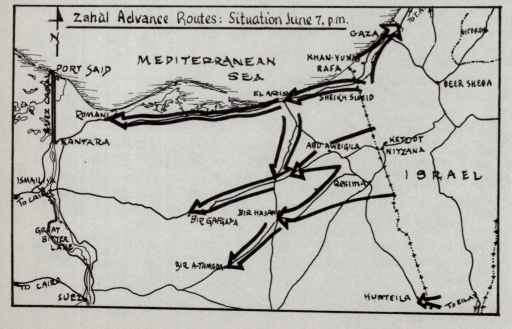

WHILE THE WEST BANK IS BEING SUBDUED, ZAHAL CONTINUES ACROSS SINAI.

offense meant toward conventional armor, had gotten hold of trumpets and ride into Jericho blaring away in the best tradition of Joshua, the son of Nun. The City of Palms is surprised by Zahal's rapid advance. Vendors abandon their stalls in the market place and flee. A Zahal unit, driving toward the Dead Sea in a commandeered Jordanian vehicle, catches up with a truckload of Legionnaires. The Jordanians are chagrined to find themselves prisoners because of an honest mistake.

The temperature stood at about 105°F. The Zahal unit continued on to Bet Haarava, the kibbutz which had attracted world attention by its success in washing the Dead Sea salts out of the soil and growing lush vegetables on the spot. The Jordanians had razed the kibbutz to the ground, progress or no progress. The old potash-producing plant was also in ruins.

With the capture of Nablus (Shechem) by Zahal, the entire West Bank was in Israel's possession. Just before the cease-fire went into effect, the bridges across the Jordan in the lower part of the valley were destroyed.

In the meantime Col. Eliezer Amitai's Jerusalem Infantry took Bethlehem and the Hebron area. Brig.-Gen. Haim Herzog was appointed Military Governor of the West Bank.

ZAHAL ARMOR SWEEPS ACROSS GEBEL-HALAL AREA,
BETWEEN QUISEMA AND BIR HASANA.

EGYPTIAN TANKS WHOOSH OUT OF SAND EMPLACE-
MENTS TO ESCAPE IAF.

DEPLOYMENT IN ANTICIPATION OF
ACTION IN GEBEL-LIBNI AREA.

A SIGHT FAMILIAR FROM 1956 DAYS: EGYPTIAN FOOTGEAR DOTS THE SINAI LANDSCAPE.

ZAHAL ARTILLERY SPEWS DESTRUCTION.

One of hundreds of Egyptian tanks left burning by Zahal action.

The Old City still has a beleaguered air about it. Shutters are drawn tight, doors are barred and bolted, stores have their grates up, the streets are deserted. The alleys are littered with empty rifle and machine-gun shells, splinters, broken glass, torn electric wires. The sewers are overflowing. On the roofs, white bits of cloth are flapping everywhere—torn underwear, strips of linen. An elderly woman in black wanders along Via Dolorosa. "Have you seen my son? A tall one with black eyes. Perhaps?"

Jerusalem is still in the midst of its celebration when another piece of good news comes through from the south: Zahal has taken Sharm-a-Sheikh. The Straits of Tiran are open! It turns out that there had been a real contest between the Navy's torpedo squadron and the paratroopers as to who would be the first to plant the Zahal flag on the squat stone building at the Straits.

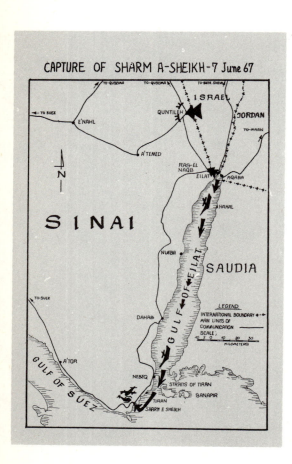

The Navy won. Later came the IAF and encircled the airfield, expecting to trap the Egyptian unit which had come in when the UNEF left, but the Egyptians were by this time in flight far up the desert.

In the large Nord transports, the paratroopers beg their commander to let them make the jump and earn the red bar for their wings. The commanders refuse, and the paratroopers are near mutiny: "What kind of war is this?"

In the hospital building, which Zahal now takes over for its headquarters, there is a goodly store of preserves, beer, blankets, communications equipment.

Chief of Operations Brig.-Gen. Ezer Weizmann arrives. He gravely notes that the Navy had taken Sharm-a-Sheikh ("I know

NAVY STEALS "MARCH" ON PARATROOPERS IN OCCUPYING SHARM-A-SHEIKH.

you had a rough time, gentlemen"). Eilat, he reports, is celebrating the opening of the Tiran Straits. The Red Sea, in comparison with the volume of toasts being exchanged by the citizens of Eilat, is a mere pond.

In northern Sinai, on this Third Day, the fighting is still very much in progress. Zahal divisions are in the midst of their maneuver to cut off the retreat routes which are already becoming clogged with fleeing Egyptian armor. Gen. Tal's division has engaged an Egyptian tank force in battle in the Bir Gafgafa area, captured the town, and has taken up positions on the surrounding hillocks. Toward midnight the Egyptians re-group and, aided by MIG's, send 60 heavy T-55's into the battle. Zahal's

light tanks duel with them for two hours. A squadron of Mirages comes overhead, clears the skies, and lets go at the Egyptian tanks.

Along the northern route, the Egyptians bring up the last of their air force in a final effort to halt the advancing Zahal column. Still, morning finds Zahal at the crossroads to Kantara, at the Canal.

Gen. Avraham Yaffe's division, having taken Bir Hasana, pushes on quickly to the Mitla Pass, one of the main routes to the Canal. Here, the IAF turns the Pass into a giant trap.

A 23-year-old Vautour flight lieutenant from Rishon Letziyon described the action:

"When I reached Mitla, I found there a

mass of burning tanks and vehicles. About a hundred tanks had bottled each other up in order to get through. We encountered no ground fire. In fact, there was not a sign of life below. The tank units had taken to the caves in the area. But our own tanks now had the problem of getting through the bottleneck. They must have used pretty big bulldozers."

The Zahal tank force did not have bulldozers. It therefore sealed off the Pass and went on along another route towards the Canal.

Gen. Ariel Sharon's division, after taking Abu-Ageila and Quesima, swung about to Kalat-a-Nahal and dug in to form a trap for the Egyptian tanks, which now had no recourse but to pass along that route. Scores of tanks are destroyed, and their crews flee into the desert.

Kuntilla and Ras-el-Nakeb fall. The burning sands of Sinai, in a seemingly endless span of time between dawn and dusk, are capable of soaking up an equally endless flow of blood.

On both sides, almost a thousand tanks had taken part in the battles. The result: a smashing victory for Israeli armor.

The general manager of Israel Railways goes to Gaza to arrange for rail service to

SHARM-A-SHEIKH AFTER ITS CAPTURE. LEFT: ISRAELI FREIGHTER "DOLPHIN" IS FIRST TO USE REOPENED STRAITS.

the Strip and El Arish . . . At the Nitzana turnoff, a young dust-covered lieutenant checks the cars. "Welcome to Egypt," he waves them on. "Today is bargain day; no visas necessary."

The reports of victories all over the Sinai Peninsula continue to pour in. Hardly possible, but there they are.

The storm clouds now shift to the north. The Syrians had moved infantry units, with tank and artillery support, against Shear-Yishuv and Tel-Dan, but were repulsed.

From the Golan Highlands comes an unremitting bombardment of the settlements below, all along the frontier. The IAF and Zahal artillery are replying.

On the diplomatic horizon, the clouds are more ominous. The Soviets have warned Israel to obey the Security Council call for a cease-fire in the area. Israel and Jordan have agreed to obey, but Egypt is still holding out; let Israel at least withdraw its forces first and be condemned as the aggressor . . .

# AT THE SUEZ CANAL

## CAPTURE OF SINAI 5-8 JUNE 67 I.D.F ROUTES OF ADVANCE

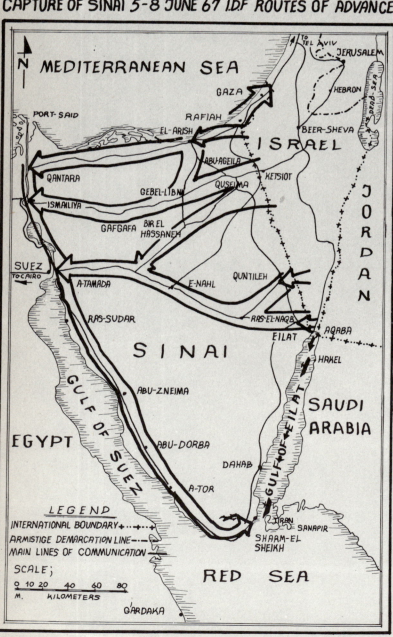

MEDITERRANEAN SEA
TO TEL AVIV
JERUSALEM
GAZA
HEBRON
PORT-SAID
RAFIAH
EL-ARISH
BEER-SHEVA
ISRAEL
QANTARA
ABU-AGEILA
KETSIOT
GEBEL-LIBNI
QUSEIMA
ISMAILIYA
GAFGAFA
BIR EL HASSANEH
SUEZ
TO-CAIRO
A-TAMADA
E-NAHL
QUNTILEH
RAS-SUDAR
RAS-EL-NAQB
AQABA
EILAT
SINAI
HAKEL
GULF OF SUEZ
GULF OF EILAT
SAUDI ARABIA
EGYPT
ABU-ZNEIMA
ABU-DORBA
DAHAB
A-TOR
TIRAN
SANAPIR
SHARM-EL SHEIKH
RED SEA
GARDAKA
JORDAN
DEAD SEA

LEGEND
INTERNATIONAL BOUNDARY +-+-+
ARMISTICE DEMARCATION LINE ---
MAIN LINES OF COMMUNICATION ==
SCALE;
0 10 20 40 60 80
M.   KILOMETERS

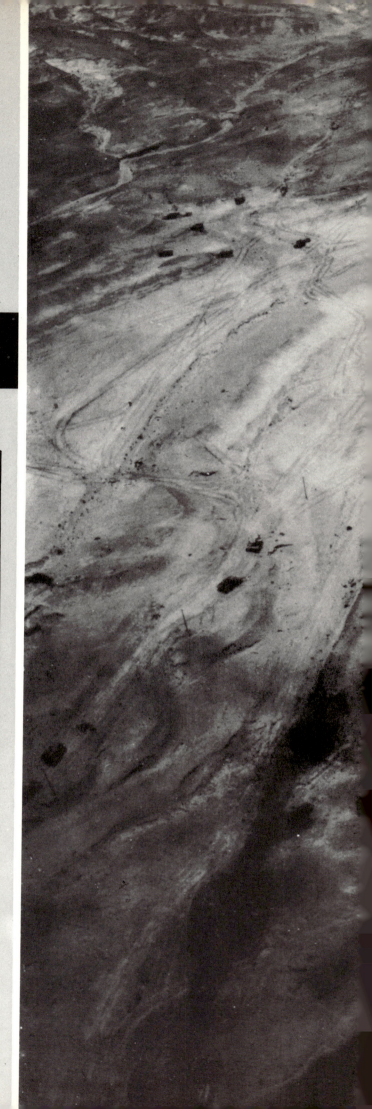

THIS was "Sinai to Suez" Day for Israel's armored divisions.

In the final drive to the Suez Canal, Gen. Tal's division split up: the southern arm took El Qantara (Kantara); the northern arm reached the Canal at a point opposite Ismailiya. The two then met on the highway parallel to the Canal.

Gen. Yaffe's division, coming from the central sector, also reached the Canal in two sections and took up positions opposite the town of Suez and Great Bitter Lake to the north of it. A force was dispatched from the Parker Monument at that point to Ras el Sudr on the shores of the Gulf of Suez. It arrived to find the area enveloped in billows of black smoke from the fires raging in the oil storage tanks; the smoke could be seen across the Peninsula. Another unit continued southward and met up, at Abu Zenima, with a detachment which had driven around the Peninsula perimeter from Sharm-a-Sheikh.

This was the last day of major warfare, and it was a bitter one. By this time the Egyptians had realized that the Zahal objective was to prevent their reaching the Canal and withdrawing to its western bank. They called on their air force to break the iron cordon, but the response was none too effective; the air force lost 2 MIG-17's, a MIG-19 and several others, including an

DEMOLISHED EGYPTIAN ARMOR BEING DRAGGED OFF THE HIGHWAY TO CLEAR WAY FOR ZAHAL'S ADVANCE.

MITLA PASS—STARK TESTIMONY TO SHATTERING BLOW DEALT EGYPT BY ZAHAL.

AIL-28 bomber. The IAF used the occasion to eliminate several batteries of SA-2 ground-to-air missiles.

IAF spotters saw below them in the desert, on this fourth day, thousands of Egyptians wandering about in search of a trail to lead them home. Behind them the vanquished Egyptians left the hulks of their vaunted Fourth Armored Division, commanded by the elite of their officers' cadre. Only a few of the finest tanks in the Division survived the duel with Gen. Tal's armor. Twisted metal bodies of Stalins and T-55's clogged the road to Ismailiya.

The war in the south was over. Gen. Yeshayahu Gavish sent Gen. Rabin a brief but significant message:

"Happy to inform you that our forces are encamped along the bank of the Suez Canal. Sinai Peninsula is in our hands. All the best to you and to Zahal."

Later, Gen. Gavish outlined the strategy of the Sinai drive, a military achievement which is likely to be studied in military academies the world over for a long time to come:

"Our first objective was to break through the Egyptians' primary line and shatter their disposition. On the second day we had to do a turnabout and destroy the enemy's attempt to prevent us from overwhelming his secondary line. On the third day, with both lines overrun and useless, we would force the Egyptians to engage us in battle. This we did by the simple maneuver of putting ourselves between them and the Canal, leaving them no choice but to fight for their lives—which they did.

"This campaign demonstrated our capacity to move fast. As for the Egyptians, they fought much better than in the Sinai Campaign of 1956. Their equipment was immeasurably superior to what they had used then. But the basic point was still there; they simply did not have the will to fight, and their commanders panicked as soon as the situation did not go by the book. It should be noted," concluded Gen. Gavish, "that Zahal routed the Egyptian army in half the time it took to do it in the Sinai Campaign of 1956."

There are now many names—Rafah, El Arish, Um-Katef—to remind Zahal men of their days of blood and sand in the desert.

Final Egyptian air attack as Zahal units near Suez.

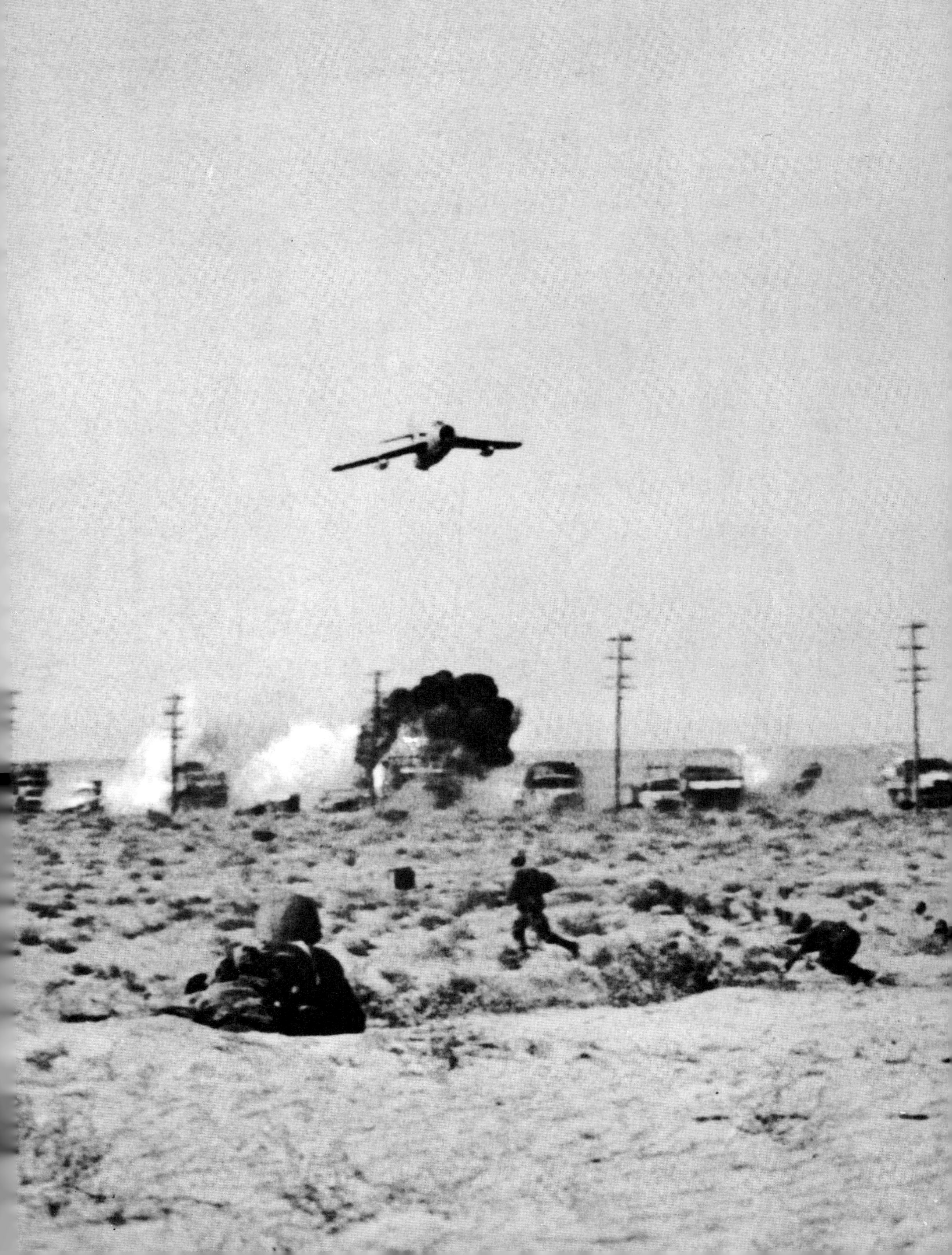

IMPRISONMENT IS STILL BETTER THAN DEATH FROM THIRST IN THE DESERT.

EGYPTIAN PRISONERS MASS BEFORE BEING TRANSFERRED TO CAMPS IN THE NORTH.

ZAHAL REACHES SUEZ CANAL IN 60 HOURS OF FIGHTING. BELOW, CENTER: SHIPS STUCK IN BITTER LAKE. LEFT: OIL TANKS AFIRE AT RAS-SUDAR.

They will long remember the concrete pill-boxes, designed by Soviet experts; the countless crates of "Semiramis" cigarettes, the huge portraits of Nasser, exhibiting the full effulgence of his white teeth. But most of all they will remember the unbelievable stocks which the Egyptians left behind; the tanks, artillery, half-tracks, missile batteries, trucks, jeeps, command cars, machine-guns, rifles and pistols of all makes. Some of the tanks were so new that they still had the original Russian markings.

There were mountainous stores to match, from blankets to Nigerian bully beef. Paris papers quoted Soviet Ambassador Zorin's report to diplomats from several "people's republics"—in three days the Egyptians lost weapons supplied to them by the Soviet Union over a period of ten years.

Three billion dollars' worth, some experts say.

Zahal soldiers treat their aching feet to a bath in the muddy waters of the Canal. Above them is the stark and sooty skeleton of the wrecked Fardan Bridge. On the opposite shore are the brownish houses and green gardens of Ismailiya. At this point the Canal is about 200 yards wide. Farther down something strange is taking place. Scores of Egyptian soldiers had succeeded in finding their way through the desert to the Canal, and now, unhindered by the Israelis, they were attempting to get back to their motherland by swimming across to the other side. However, Egyptians stationed on the west bank are shooting at them, in the water. Consensus of the Zahal spectators is that Nasser does not want to have the story of the Egyptian military debacle spread throughout the land.

Egypt now agreed to the cease-fire. Syria, Iraq, Algeria and Kuwait declared that they were still at war with Israel.

The Egyptian propaganda machine was now confronted with the unenviable task of explaining away Egypt's military disaster. It came up with a "lulu"; the High Command, said Cairo Radio and press, is in possession of "incontrovertible evidence" that U.S. and British planes, taking off from the U.S. air base in Libya and the decks of U.S. 6th Fleet aircraft carriers,

had helped Israel in the air battles and provided an aerial umbrella for Zahal operations. The U.S. and Britain vehemently denied the charge; the Soviet Union, knowing the score, made no comment. Israel then offered in evidence the tape of a conversation between Nasser and Hussein which laid the egg of the alleged "U.S.–British intervention".

The fourth day was not without its grievous incident. At night Israeli torpedo boats and planes attacked an unidentified craft off the coast opposite El Arish. The craft had refused to reveal its identity. Later it was discovered that this was the *Liberty*, a U.S. communications vessel. The attack caused 35 deaths; more than a hundred were wounded. The Israel Government apologized to the U.S. and expressed its regrets.

Comments from abroad on Israel's victory glowed with enthusiasm. "The most legendary victory in history" — "The most brilliant military campaign in all history" — "Not the Great Powers but the Israeli soldiers provided the decisive action to assure international peace." British Intelligence claimed that it was the accuracy on the part of its Israeli counterpart, in pinpointing the location of all those Egyptian air bases, which turned the tide so early and so decisively. An Italian newspaper noted that Nasser had poured the billions given him by nations all around the globe into armaments, instead of providing aid for his impoverished farmers. Thousands throughout Italy donate blood for Israel. Artists, authors and academicians, sign declarations and petitions, address public gatherings, offer aid to Israel. An Italian merchant marine captain, age 70, telephones to the Jewish Agency office in Genoa: "It is true that I am on in years, but my hands are still good and I can do whatever you will ask of me."

King Hussein of Jordan, he who had gambled and lost, appeared at his first press conference of the war. Sorrowfully he admitted: "Despite their heroic efforts to protect our soil, our forces were routed by the Israeli army. Our losses are very high. We fought with no chance of succeeding. The Israeli planes rained down destruction upon all our units. Jordan was deserted completely by its friends." The Jordanian Government also admitted, officially, that no U.S. or British aircraft had fought against Jordan.

Israel now faced up to the responsibility of setting its house in order. The Ramallah station took over *Kol Yisrael*'s regular broadcasts in Arabic. "Egged" Bus No. 9 resumed its route to Mount Scopus. Old-timers who were brutally forced to give up their homes in Gush Etzyon, in the Hebron area in 1948, now petitioned the Government to allow their sons to resettle there.

But in the north, along the Syrian Highlands, the shelling was still going on.

----

# WEST BANK OPENS UP

## SYRIAN ATTACKS 5-9 JUNE 67

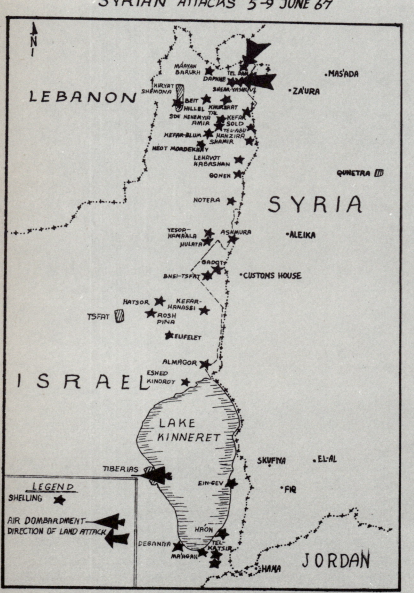

N

LEBANON

MA'AYAN BARUKH
KIRYAT SHEMONA
DAPHNE
TEL DAN
SHEAR-YASHUV
•MAS'ADA
•ZA'URA
BEIT HILLEL
TAL
KHURSHAT
SDE NEHEMYA
AMIR
KEFAR SOLD
TEL-ABU HANZIRA
KEFAR-BLUM
NEOT MORDEKHAY
SHAMIR
LEHAVOT HABASHAN
QONEN
QUNETRA
NOTERA
SYRIA
YESOD-HAMA'ALA
HULATA
ASHMURA
•ALEIKA
GADOT
BNEI-TSFAT
•CUSTOMS HOUSE
HATSOR
KEFAR-HANASSI
TSFAT
ROSH PINA
ELIFELET
ALMAGOR
ESHED KINOROT
ISRAEL
LAKE KINNERET
TIBERIAS
EIN-GEV
SKUFNA
•EL-AL
•FIQ
HAON
DEGANYA
TEL-KATSIR
MA'AGAN
HAMA
JORDAN

### LEGEND
SHELLING ★

AIR BOMBARDMENT
DIRECTION OF LAND ATTACK

IN the southern and central sectors, the shooting has died down. The West Bank is showing signs of readiness to adapt itself to the Israeli scene. The holy sites, Gen. Haim Herzog assures religious dignitaries in the Old City, will be scrupulously guarded by special Zahal units. Speaking for the church hierarchy, Greek Orthodox Archbishop Benedictus replies, first in English then in Greek: "We are not politicians! We are men of the cloth and all we ask is that we be allowed to live in accordance with our faith and to fulfill the commandments of our religion. I wish to acknowledge, at this time, with deep gratitude, that the Israeli army did no damage to our holy places in the course of the battle."

Three Jordanian newsmen offer to put out a daily "as soon as tomorrow." Their senior, Yussuf Hanna, shakes hands with Jewish colleagues of former years.

In Hebron, the Cave of Machpela is open to Jews for the first time in a hundred years. Heretofore, Jews had not been permitted to ascend above the seventh step leading to the Mosque of Ibrahim, erected on the base of the Cave.

Zahal soldiers stand in line to see the reputed tombs of Abraham and Sarah; the cover, of green velvet, is embroidered with Arabic characters in gold. Hebron Mayor Sheikh Muhammad Jabr, thrice a minister in the Jordanian Government, publicly thanks Israel's Government for its promise to safeguard the holy places and see to the welfare of the residents of the West Bank. Hebron, in 1929, perpetrated a horrible massacre of its Jewish residents.

Visitors flock again to Rachel's Tomb in Bethlehem. Chief Chaplain Goren has already emptied the Holy Ark of its accumulation of old Arab newspapers, and has placed in it a Scroll of the Law. Above the police building, a makeshift Israeli flag—a bedsheet with a blue Star of David roughly inked in—flutters in the breeze. In the center of the town, one of the major attractions for Christian tourists, young vendors of souvenirs swarm about the Zahal soldiers, offering beads, postcards,

WEST BANK GOVERNOR, BRIG.-GEN. HAIM HERZOG (CENTER).

stamps, shoe-shines. Peddlers pass with carts of coffee, peanuts and "Lulu" brand Jordanian cigarettes. Israeli currency is just fine, and the official rate of exchange is known by all.

Jericho, city of palms, bananas and hot springs, is back to normal; people wave to Zahal trucks passing by. Ramallah, Sheikh-Jarrah and Bet-Hanina no longer resemble a battlefield; stores let down their shutters, slowly, gingerly. Here and there a pyjama-clad Legionnaire or a sniper is led away to the prisoners' compound. Zahal sappers are ceaselessly dismantling acres of booby-traps.

Col. Shlomo Lahat, governor of the Jerusalem area, issues an order, in no uncertain terms; any Zahal member caught looting would face court martial. Local police constables and municipal workers have been asked to return to their jobs. Jerusalem Mayor Teddy Kollek instructs his municipal agencies to extend their services to the Old City and the liberated suburbs. Several weddings have already taken place at the Western Wall.

While Zahal is recovering its breath in

THE C-O-S AND GEN. NARKISS VISIT CHURCH.

PILGRIMS VISIT MACHPELA CAVE IN HEBRON.

Sinai and along the central front, the situation in the north is becoming more serious. Syrian artillery, reports a Zahal commander, is now "firing hysterically." The old settlement of Rosh-Pinna has absorbed, in forty minutes, some one thousand shells from long-range guns, heavy mortars, and Russian "Katyushas".

The IAF is called in. Vautour assault bombers rake the Syrians' rear lines, along the Damascus–Kuneitra line. Reported Lieutenant Zeev, reservist, a test pilot for Aircraft Industries: "We came in easily and set ourselves up, since there were no enemy planes to deter us and no anti-aircraft fire to speak of. We dived, one after the other, counting up our direct hits."

At 11:30 a.m. of Friday, June 9, Zahal went on the offensive. The news was flashed all along the battered valley: "Zahal is going atop the Golan!"

Zahal had decided on the northern approach to the Syrian dispositions as the point for the breakthrough attempt. After a basic softening of the Syrian positions by the Air Force, Col. Albert's armored brigade was given the command to storm the Highlands, bristling with reinforced concrete pillboxes and equipped with enormous quantities of the latest Soviet arms.

Exposed to a withering fire, the Engineers Corps advanced steadily, hammering out a path along the rocky slope for the advance of the armored columns, which clambered up at a point opposite Kfar Szold and fronting the Syrian positions at Neamush. The armored force split up, one proceeding to Zeura and the other to Zu'eib-el-Mis. Zeura was taken at four in the afternoon, and the column moved south to join the other arm. By evening the operation was over.

An infantry force of the Golani Border Troops, under the command of Col. Yonah, went up for the attack on the almost impregnable positions at Tel Aziziat, Tel Fahr, Burj-Babil and Banias Village. These positions were impervious to armor. The Syrians were entrenched in bunkers gouged out of the mountainside and connected with one another by concrete-lined trenches. As an added precaution, a forest of barbed wire had been strung in front of the fortifications.

Prime Minister Levi Eshkol and Minister Menachem Begin visit with victorious units.

A WEDDING AT THE WESTERN WALL. WHAT A PHOTOGRAPH FOR THE CHILDREN AND GRANDCHILDREN!

Russian SA2 missile base taken by Zahal armor.

KIBBUTZ HOUSES DAMAGED; SHELTERS PROTECTED
INHABITANTS.

ROSH-PINNA SUFFERED HEAVY DAMAGE.

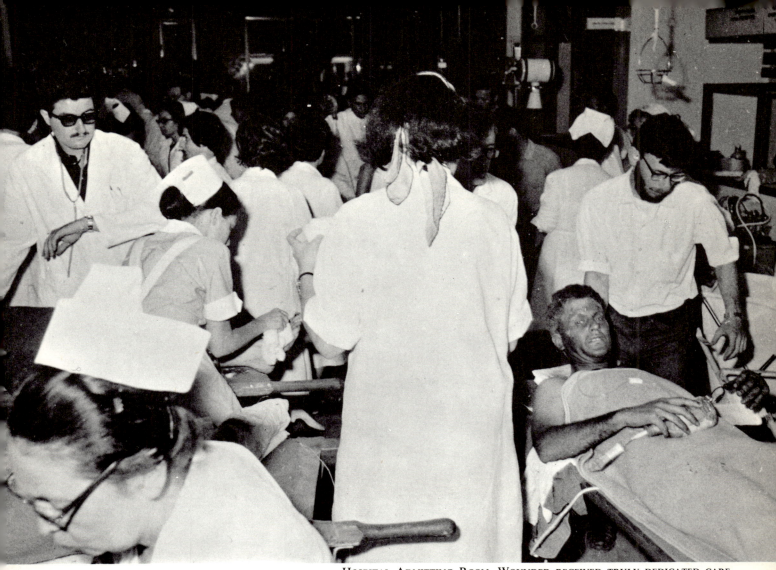

HOSPITAL ADMITTING ROOM. WOUNDED RECEIVED TRULY DEDICATED CARE.

HOUSEWIFE ATTEMPTS TO PUT OUT FIRE CAUSED BY SHELLING.

As the Golani were about to begin their climb, Col. Yonah said to them: "I know that we have a difficult assignment. Our objectives are tough and well-fortified, but I have no doubt that you will carry out the assignment as is expected of you."

The ascent began. First went the armored force, then the Golani in the half-tracks. Jurj-Babil, on the outer fringe, was taken at once. Now Tel Fahr loomed ahead—an intricate network of concrete trenches with impenetrable walls, built like an underground fortress.

Here took place one of the bloodiest battles of the war, hours on end of hand-to-hand fighting. The Golani forked out, attacking from directly below the positions and flanking them on the south, cutting through the barbed wire under the very muzzles of the Syrian machine-guns.

One of the Golani described it: "We stormed the Syrian positions. They crouched low in the trenches; didn't even stick their noses out. Each of us went in on his own, first with grenades, then with all the ammunition in our Uzzis, followed by

ISRAELI SOLDIER HELPS ARAB MOTHER AT ALLENBY BRIDGE ON WAY TO AMMAN.

commando knives. We had to clean out the trenches yard by yard."

The commander of the advance unit told further: "I had just gotten into the pillbox when I saw a Syrian officer coming. I pressed the trigger, but there were no more bullets left. For a moment we stood there looking at each other. He then tried to fire his pistol at me. I threw myself at him. We both rolled along the bottom of the trench. I felt a terrible blow on my arm. The Syrian hit me on the head with his pistol and I tried a stranglehold on him. At this point one of my men came along but had to hold his fire because the two of us were entangled. I succeeded in throwing him off, and a bullet finished him. I grabbed his pistol and went on to the next position. I still think that, had I not been wounded in the thigh earlier, I could have taken care of the situation."

The battle for Tel Fahr ended with nightfall. The Golani continued to comb the positions meticulously; in many cases the Syrians would draw back into a corner to give the impression that the bunker had been abandoned, and then open fire at the backs of the Israeli soldiers. Other Syrians, wounded, hoisted white flags and were taken prisoner; moments later, they produced pistols hidden in their uniforms and shot their captors from behind.

The Golani, never slackening the pace of their attack, captured Urfeiya, opposite Notera, and opened the way for the armored brigade which cut through as far as Roya Village. Infantry and paratrooper units went on to crack the Syrian defense installations, capturing Gelabina, Dardara, Tel Hilal and Darbashiya—the positions which had for years rained destruction down on the settlements in the valley.

Zahal took advantage of the darkness to fuel up, replenish provisions, and re-group for the next day's fighting. Below them, the settlers of Upper Galilee remained underground in their shelters, listening, with hope and trepidation, to the erupting highlands of the Golan.

◄ IMPROMPTU MONUMENT TO ADVANCE UNIT'S FALLEN.

# ATOP THE GOLAN

162

THE sixth and last day of the war fell on the Sabbath, but for Zahal it was anything but a day of repose. The battle with the Syrians was resumed at daybreak, at the same pace of the previous day. The armored force under the command of Lieut.-Col. Moshe attacked the Syrian positions at Tel-Hamra, helped take Banias village, cleaned out Nubeila, then went back east and took part in subduing Mas'eda. Col. Albert's armored brigade sped toward Mansura–Kuneitra.

Kuneitra, the last bastion, fell at 2:30 in the afternoon after twenty-four hours of fighting, and the Golan Highlands were in Zahal's hands. One could almost sense the sigh of relief that went up from the harrassed settlements in the valley, from Tel-Dan in the north to Almagor in the south. Overnight the Syrian nightmare had been dispelled. Brig.-Gen. David Elazar, head of the Northern Command, summing up the Golan Highlands campaign, attributed the successful onslaught of his men on the unusually well-fortified positions of the enemy to three factors:

MOBILE FORCE CROSSES BNOT YAAQOV BRIDGE.

ZAHAL ARMOR SWEEPS AWAY SYRIAN POSITIONS, BANE OF VALLEY SETTLERS FOR 19 YEARS.

the highly-efficient battle tactics of the Israel Air Force; the imbalance into which the enemy forces had been thrown by Zahal's bold and unexpected methods of attack, and the early desertion of the Syrian officers from the fighting area, leaving their men in a state of panic; the number of Syrian officers among the captives was relatively small.

Zahal losses in the struggle for the Highlands came to 115 dead and 105 wounded. In the Jordanian sector, Zahal lost 107 men, while the wounded amounted to 322.

The summary of the southern campaign was given by Gen. Yeshayahu Gavish, head of the Southern Command, and Generals Tal, Yaffe and Sharon. Gen. Gavish:

"We had a three-fold objective in the south—one, to destroy the Egyptian army, once and for all; two, to capture the Straits of Tiran and Sharm-a-Sheikh and open the waterways to Eilat; three, in order to achieve the second objective, to take all of the Sinai Peninsula.

"As to the description of the course of events: The first stage began when I was informed, at 8:00 a.m., that the enemy had launched his attack. We went forth to meet him in preventive action at 8:15, proceeding along two routes: one, Khan-Yunis–Rafah in the direction of El Arish; two, Ktziot–Abu-Ageila. A full division operated along each route. At the same time, a third division, moving along dirt roads, broke into the center of the Gebel-Libni–Bir Gafgafa–Bir Lahfan area. In this stage, which was completed on the morning of the next day, we captured El Arish and Abu-Ageila, where we now had stationed a full division. We completed taking the Gaza Strip.

"In the second stage, we moved on to crack the enemy's secondary line of defense, between Gebel-Libni and Bir Hasana, and Gen. Yaffe's division accomplished this assignment most commendably. Gen. Tal's division made a quick breakthrough at Bir Lahfan on the north. Gen. Sharon's division took Quseima.

"The third stage was armor against armor. We surrounded the enemy and forced him into battle. The fighting continued during the entire day and part of the night. About a thousand tanks in all took part in this engagement, which ended about ten o'clock at night. At three in the morning our forces reached the Suez Canal. On the same day our paratroopers and naval forces landed at Sharm-a-Sheikh, and an overland force reached Ras-Sudar via Mitla Pass.

"The results of the campaign in the south: Some 600 Egyptian tanks were destroyed, and a hundred tanks fell into our hands intact. About ten thousand Egyptians were killed, thousands taken prisoner, and tens of thousands are wandering toward the Canal. Our losses: 275 dead, 800 wounded, 61 tanks hit.

"Now these are the conclusions to be derived from the campaign: In four days less five hours, the Israeli force of three divisions vanquished and shattered seven

AFTER SOFTENING SYRIAN POSITIONS (RIGHT), ZAHAL TANKS HEAD FOR GOLAN HIGHLANDS.

Egyptian divisions. This came about because of several factors: first, the concentration of our forces, swift mobility and maintenance of impetus. We fought four days and nights without letup. Secondly, the officers set the pace of the fighting. Many of our casualties were officers, commanders of companies, battalions, even brigades.

"The quality of the soldiers, both the regulars and the reserves, was eminently high. Their courage was unbelievable. We used unconventional methods of penetration to undermine, in the very beginning, the fighting potential of the

ISRAELI TANKS CROSS CROSS NORTHERN BORDER.

AFTER THE CONQUEST, A SNAPSHOT AT BANIAS SPRING.

SYRIANS ROUTED, ZAHAL UNIT COMBS AREA.

KUNEITRA CITIZENRY HAS FLED TO DAMASCUS.

enemy. The organization of our maintenance system enabled the divisions to function independently for seventy two hours, and replenishments were called for on the last day only. Our air advantage was a most important factor, enabling us as it did to move about freely and according to plan.

"As for the enemy. The Egyptians were equipped with the finest weapons and armament. Their stocks were full. They fought well on defense, less efficiently when they were on the move, but collapsed completely when they had to match our pace and the fighting conditions which we set.

"Finally, this war was truly a people's struggle, carried out by the citizens who mobilized and carried it out with body and spirit. As for the division commanders, Generals Tal, Yaffe and Sharon—with three such generals you can get very far."

On the Syrian Highlands and all over Sinai, Zahal captured hundreds, perhaps thousands, of all kinds of field pieces, among them the "Awesome Katyusha", manned by a crew of six, which fires 32 rockets at once at objectives some 9,000 yards distant; new 122 mm. howitzers and 130 mm. shore batteries. In Sinai, Zahal also came across and retained three kinds of missiles: two-stage ground-to-air Soviet SAM's, which travel at four times the speed of sound, at a height of up to 60,000 feet; the SAMAL anti-tank missile with an operational range of up to 2,500 yards; AA2 air-to-air missiles used by MIG-21's. There were amphibious tanks, the latest in communications equipment, myriads of "Gurinov" machine-guns, "Port Said" sub-machine guns and IK54 rifles, hundreds of BTR-152 armored troop transports, ZFO heavy anti-aircraft artillery, Soviet ZIL trucks with self-sealing tires, spare parts without number, gas warfare equipment and thousands of tins of canned meat from China (the last in Syrian bunkers).

On Monday, June 12, 1967, the Chief of Staff, Major-General Yitzhak Rabin, issued, from the Western Wall, the following Order of the Day:

"Soldiers of Zahal! Now, with the cease-fire, there comes to an end the struggle we have waged against those who would have shrouded us with oblivion.

"The Israel Defense Forces, on land, sea and in the air, have shattered the armies of four Arab states. Undivided Jerusalem is free. The West Bank is in our hands. The entire Sinai Peninsula is under our control. The Syrian threat to the northern settlements has been banished.

"The war was not an easy one. It was waged by Zahal—and Zahal alone. The battles spread over wide areas. All the forces of Zahal, the regulars and the reserves, the border settlements and the home front—all have a share in this great endeavor.

"Many of our commanders and soldiers have fallen in battle. We shall remember the with sorrow—and pride.

"Zahal has carried out all of its assignments, with the power of the supreme effort on the part of its commanders and soldiers—and the pace of its operations.

"The struggle may not yet be over. I want to state here, at the Western Wall, with full confidence, that as we went forth to

ROAD TO KUNEITRA LITTERED WITH CHARRED REMAINS OF SYRIAN ARMOR.

fight for these achivements, so we shall know how to safeguard and protect them in the future.

"Commanders and soldiers—we salute you!"

The Six-Day War had come to an end. The tortuous borders have been straightened. The weather forecast now announces the degree of humidity on the Golan Highlands, Solomon's Straits, Gaza, northern Sinai. The sands of Sinai are still strewn with the twisted wreckage of a oncemighty war machine. Hundreds of homes in Israel are in silent mourning. Medals and citations will have to be distributed to thousands. Hundreds of tales of valor are yet to be told—the Navy operation in the harbor of Port Said, for instance—but this is a task for the historians. For only they, aided by the perspective of time, will be able to plumb, fathom and assess the full measure of those great moments, the glory-crowned hours of the Six-Day War of 1967.

IN THE VALLEY BELOW THE GOLAN HIGHLANDS, ALL IS CALM.